Spirit Nudges

Proof That Spirit Is Never Far Away

Story & Original Paintings
By Michelle Rathore

Squiggle Publishing
United Kingdom

ISBN: ebook 978-0-9572267-1-5
ISBN: print 978-0-9572267-2-2

Published by:
Squiggle Publishing
72 Richmond Street
Ashton-Under-Lyne
Lancashire, OL6 7BJ
United Kingdom
Telephone +44 161 343 3833
Fax +44 161 343 3633
www.squigglepublishing.com
Cover: Original Photo© Michelle Rathore

I, Michelle Rathore, do hereby swear the cover photo to be a truephoto which has not been altered in any way to mislead anyone.
The sleeping gentleman is my Dad: Michael B. Ward Sr. Photo taken at my home,personally—by me, in England. Photo used with permission. Thanks Dad!
In Chapter 9: Heaven—and Back! You can read all about my Dad and this amazing photograph!

Dedication

To the Light within us all, may it burn brightly on your
darkest day to show you the way home.

Rest assured; you never walk alone.

In memory of our little sister:
Michawn Lynnette Ward
(Feb. 21, 1973 – Dec. 16, 1989)

and

Marcus Andrew Wehmeyer
(March 15, 1987)

...they live on.

Acknowledgements

I want to thank my wonderful family and friends who proof-read many many edits and constantly encouraged me the whole way. My parents, Michael Ward Sr. and Mary Lou Ward who continue to believe me and in me. To Dad for allowing me to use his 'sleeping' picture. My brother Michael Ward Jr. and sister-in-law Tammy Ward for their continued love and support. Friends Michelle Halliwell, Pauline Rogers, Angela Kay and Bill Foss who gave loads of good advice and helped polish the mirror in front of me. My amazing children P.J. Wehmeyer, Xara, Rocco and Marcus Rathore who are a constant source of love and inspiration to me. Of course my wonderful husband Ajaz Rathore whose bucket of love and support seems to never run empty. Indeed Great Spirit for allowing me to be a part of your tremendous plan.

Contents

"And behold, I AM with you always....."
The Bible

Matthew 28:20

Preface

From my earliest memories in childhood I've been able see and hear spirit. I thought it was just normal and everyone could so I never found the need to ask anyone about it. I grew up in a smallish town in the southern part of Texas. My family went to church regularly and I listened with great interest when the preacher would talk about the Holy Spirit and how people in the olden days would be visited by Angels and given all this amazing information that was written down and handed back to us as 'The Bible'. I wondered if there were still people who were doing that now as I knew the Angels were still visiting us or had we already written everything down that they had to tell us. I was probably like a lot of children who are just waiting complacently for life to happen to them. I don't think I was ever really an active participant in life. I was just 'waiting to grow up' and since no one ever talked about being able to see or hear what I was experiencing I reasoned maybe I shouldn't talk about it either. Actually I don't think it was ever a conscious decision on my part to hide my gifts. I just seemed to live in my own little cocoon and pretty much still do to this day. I am an active observer.

As it happens I did grow up and when I hit my 20's I finally reached a point that I had so much going on with the spirit world and I really didn't understand most of it. One day I decid-

ed to tell my Mother about some of the things I was experiencing. For one thing I could hear people talking when there was
no one around. And for another thing I was discovering more
and more gifts that I had been blissfully ignorant of up to that
point. At the time I didn't know what clairvoyance, clairaudi-
ence or claire-cognizance was. I needed to put a label on what
was happening to me. Maybe I was testing the water to see if
this part of my reality would be accepted as I was having more
and more very vivid dreams that were coming true and I needed
someone to help me understand what, if anything, it all meant. I
was having regular visitation from Spirit and I had no clue what
they wanted. Sometimes they would just stand next to my bed
and look at me. What were they looking at? What did they want?
How was I to know?

As my Mother didn't really know what to tell me about what
I was experiencing she confided in one of my aunts for council.
The answer came back from this relative that what I was experiencing was 'the Devil trying to get me' and that I shouldn't listen
to the voices I was hearing. So, as you might imagine, I went back
into hiding to learn what I could on my own for fear of ridicule
from the outside world. I didn't want people to think I was working with the Devil. This was part of the Bible belt and everyone knew if you were working with the devil you would burn in
Hell!! Nothing could have been further from the truth. I wasn't
working with anyone – I didn't know *how* and that pretty much
was the biggest problem for me. I had no control over anything
that was happening and that included the precognitive dreams I
was continuing to experience on a more and more regular basis.
In fact, it was the precognitive dreams that sent me looking for
deeper answers after I saw my sister's death two weeks before it
happened. The guilt of not understanding my gifts was almost
unbearable to me. So, through my self-imposed guilt, I began
to study in private trying earnestly to learn all I could about the
gifts people have and how I might use them for a higher purpose.
I needed to find out how I might be able to use the gifts that were

emerging to try and save someone else if I did have another pre-cognitive dream. What I was to find out over the coming years led me far from home – to another continent and to multiple dimensions of time and space. I hope you will keep an open mind while reading the pages of my life so far on this journey. I can't hide any longer – my children have the same gifts and I have to offer them what knowledge I have learned, so far, on my journey.

This is a true story but I have had to change a few names to offer privacy to a couple of individuals. I hope this book warms your heart and helps you embrace all that you truly are as well as reminding you of the existence of spirit helpers, angels, guides and all beings of light and to lift you to a new level of understanding who you really are.

"A journey of a thousand miles begins with a single step."

—Lao-tzu
(604 BC - 531 BC)
Chinese Philosopher

1. Kitchen Helper

I was in the kitchen that sunny afternoon getting dinner ready for the family. I was enjoying the quiet of an empty house and the hum of the overhead extractor fan as the children played outside in the sun. The French doors were wide open and leading out to the garden. It was a little too cold to have the doors open but I liked the fresh blasts of wind now and again so I left them latched open anyway. I stopped for a moment to admire the magnificent view we enjoy overlooking the English countryside before going back to the stove to continue cooking. Trying to keep the pots bubbling away seemed futile with the wind blowing its rhythmic blasts of fresh air all the way across the kitchen. Finally, the flames on the stove could stand no more wind and I was forced to close the doors. Having unlatched and closed both large glass French doors I walked back around the end of the counter toward the stove and as I did I noticed a little visitor who came walking in from the open hallway door.

Sitting down at the breakfast bar, which could seat all five of our family at once, she chose the seat right in the middle as though this comforted her in some way. This five or six year old, dark haired girl with pigtails tied in ribbons, was worried about her mother and wanted to talk to me about it. I intuitively understood her name was Lizzie. I continued to cook – and listen.

Lizzie began sending images to my mind. This is one of the ways Spirit can communicate with us. It's like watching someone else's memories play in my own mind and I don't really know if they are transmitting their own thoughts to me or if they are able to mesh their thoughts with my own in a way that just looks like someone playing a movie in my head. Perhaps we will know one day the true mechanics of it all but, all that matters is that she was able to relate to me a message. Lizzie showed me her mother and another woman, a dear relative or friend no doubt, who were crying and holding on to each other as to comfort one another. I felt Lizzie had left home one morning a very long time ago and never came back. And, tragically, I also felt she had never been found.

As I stood watch over my bubbling pots, Lizzie seemed quite content to connect with me in this way so I quite naturally allowed my mind to connect with her energy and listened. She showed me that she had gone out to play with a neighbor boy who was in his late teens but had the mind of a much younger person. They played and ran through tall grass and down a little hill where many thin trees began to shoot up and then lead into a kind of overgrowth. This was a little farther than Lizzie was supposed to stray away from her home but she was having fun and the time just seemed to slip away. Evening was setting in Lizzie's story as she showed me what happened next. The focus turned to the feeling of a type of falling or tripping sensation and it was as if I was now looking through Lizzie's eyes. I was going head first down the hill toward a tree. I was moving too fast to stop and the tree was getting closer quicker. My heart was racing. Then, everything went black. Everything was silent for a very short time and then it was as if I was standing – but more like floating – and I was there next to Lizzie on the ground all bundled in a heap at the base of a tree. As I looked up a very bright light came slowly moving from the woods toward me and as it got closer the light gradually built in intensity and brilliance. I was not afraid or should I say, Lizzie was not afraid. I was again watching as Lizzie showed me that she was met by a brilliant light body. This Light body was full of love and warmth and made her feel completely at ease. Lizzie had felt no pain just before passing over to spirit and she felt no fear when she was met by this Angel of Love. This was the message she was trying to get into my head and into her mother's heart. This is what she desperately needed her mother to know.

Lizzie didn't want to talk anymore about how she had died. She just said, "It was an accident. He didn't mean to hurt me. I just died and he panicked. He cried a long time and then dug a hole and put me in it. He was very kind to me. And then he went home."

Lizzie had pretty much just told me she had died accidentally and been buried by a mentally handicapped neighbor boy. She wanted her mother to know she was alright and that she didn't want her to cry anymore.

I asked Lizzie if I knew her mother. She sat there at my kitchen table with her hands clasped in front of her; head bowed and did not reply. I asked her if I would be able to tell her mother, one day, this message she had just given me. She looked up and smiled at me. Lizzie excitedly shook her head 'Yes' – in her red and white check dress with those dark curly pigtails – she began to fade from my sight. The sound of the overhead extractor fan seemed to get a bit louder. My attention refocused as I went back to one of the French doors, opened it, and shouted outside to my own children who were still playing in the sun, "Come eat – dinner's ready."

This sort of visitation has been a regular occurrence for me from the time I was very young and continues today. It doesn't scare me, in fact, it just feels normal now. It's a very real part of who I am. The older I get the more I find I need to write things down. Some of the stories – like the ones I will share with you here – never needed writing down as they are etched in my memory forever.

"You have to leave the city of your comfort and go into the wilderness of your intuition.

What you'll discover will be wonderful. What you'll discover is yourself."

—Alan Alda(1936 -)
American Actor

2. A Little Courage Can Be Dangerous

On my journey I have found that I tend to read as much as I can on the subject of psychics and mediumship. It's not so much just a fascination with the subject I am living but also a way of trying to find out how others with my gifts have managed to develop their own gifts and apply them to their lives. Many years ago, having devoured the latest edition of *'No Don't Do It That Way – Do It This Way'*, I found myself taking to heart a bit of advice that was given in this particular text book. It was pointed out that if you had read through the entire book and found yourself to have many of the qualities that were indicated in the text as being 'extra-ordinary' then you should take yourself by the hand and go straight to the first Spiritualist Church you could find. The author was even kind enough to say, "Tell them I sent you." Oh good - a recommendation! I was soon to find that years of hiding my gifts and learning in secret had made me a bit paranoid, to say the least.

Well, being the sensible person I am I got straight on the internet and found a wide and varied list of Spiritualist Churches in Northern England. True to form, nothing is easy! Scrolling through all the choices and clicking myself silly my eyes began to glaze over with all the 'truth' I was able to locate. I decided the best course of action would be to just go to whichever facility was closest to my home. And that is exactly what I did.

Locating a website that had a searchable database I quickly found my local Spiritualist church. My hands were shaking with the excited realization that I had finally located a place I could go that wasn't actually too far away. I went out determined to have, at the very least, a good drive past the location to see if everything was 'OK' if you know what I mean. It was mid afternoon, a sunny day. I had the cover of the darkened windows in my car to obscure me from anyone's sight that might be walking past. In my own mind I was relatively safe.

I went to the general location which was, surprisingly, given quite openly on the website and began to drive down the side streets as I figured they must have to stash themselves away to avoid the tyrannical villagers with pitchforks and torches blazing on darkened nights trying to appease their appetites with the self-righteous annihilation of those who are strange or different and sometimes referred to as 'freaks'.

I began to get edgy. I must be getting close. Yes, there was the building standing quietly on the corner trying to look normal. I could tell though. I could see past it's freshly painted walls. Someone must be near writing down license plates of passers-by. Was it all an elaborate setup to sniff out the last of us who didn't really know there's no such thing as being special or gifted? Would this be the last time I would be seen? I remembered just then that I had not left a note at home to say where I was going. Would I just disappear and be an addition to the next Crime Watch program?

"Yes, she seemed a normal enough lady. Michelle Rathore was last seen driving past the Hyde Spiritual Center on Monday afternoon. Witnesses say she drove slowly along the road and down the lane where she seemed to evaporate into thin air."

I was sure I could smell a faint kerosene scent in the air.

Were the angry villagers waiting in ambush for me to stop my vehicle and naively get out and have a look?

I drove past again and thought it was a bit funny that there was no one there! I slowed down and checked the address again on the scribbled piece of paper, which was now damp from being clasped in my anxious fist and drove by once more, this time checking the shrubs for beady eyes following my movements. I was disgusted! I had worked up the nerve to track them down and there was not a soul around. So, what did I do? Yes, that's right. I stopped the car. After being so careful as to not be noticed – I parked right out in front of the building- and got out. There was a note on the door. I just knew they had left it for me. Can you imagine my surprise when I discovered the note really *was* for me – and anyone else who wanted to read it? Absorbing the encrypted message I quickly determined several vital clues. I was there on the wrong day, at the wrong time and had to remember when planning my next visit that I must not go on an evening that was 'FOR MEMBERS ONLY'.

I was slapped into touch rather quickly. After all that commotion I found out they were operating out in the public for all to witness. Suddenly, I didn't need my sunglasses anymore. The air seemed a bit fresher but I still wondered – what did they do differently on the night that was designated for members only?

I did eventually find a church to go to but, of course, the search for truth is often fraught with obstacles as I was soon to find out – again.

As I was very intent on developing my gifts and being aware that a lot of people also call them 'skills' I thought it would be a good idea to learn how to meditate properly. Surely this would help me quiet my mind and assist in finding the direction I should take. At the very least I would be getting out of the house one evening a week and have the satisfaction of knowing I was at least trying to better myself. I felt a lot less apprehensive about going to a class when a friend of mine told me her dad was starting a new meditation class and I was welcome to come along. Well I was thrilled! Just the ticket! I found out when the first class was scheduled and couldn't wait for the day to come around. Spirit must be helping me once again – I was positive of it.

It was a few days until time for the scheduled meditation class to begin and as each day passed I curiously found myself becoming more and more filled with a mixture of excitement and trepidation. The day finally rolled around and I made sure I was on time to the class which hosted about eight other people along with the instructor – my friend's dad. He was a very pleasant looking older gentleman with a vitality not often seen in people his age. He seemed to have a peacefulness residing in him that I was hoping to locate within myself and use in working more closely with the spirit world. If I am honest I had placed a lot of expectation on that one meditation class. I was hoping to find guidance and direction which could assist me in moving forward with my gifts in a way I could more easily control at will. Looking back I know, in the early days, I was like an antenna walking around just receiving absolutely everything that was around me. I was like a sponge non-discriminately soaking up everything from the spirit world and I was being silently guided to find a better way of operating as being an open receiver all the time can be very exhausting and quite confusing too.

I was happy it was a small class and we were asked to each find a chair and get comfortable. We were told that at this first meeting we would just be quieting our mind and then, later, we would have the opportunity for discussion if we wanted to but, this would be in private with the instructor who had been a practicing Buddhist for many, many years. I was quite happy with what was explained to me and so we began the task of quieting our minds.

We sat in a circle in folding chairs. I could hear other people breathing deeply in and then out. Over and over again, rhythmically, breathing deeply. Some were breathing so deeply in and out it almost sounded like they were wheezing. I wondered to myself if that sort of wheezing deep breathing was really helping them to quiet their mind or where they just pretending to be deep breathing? My attention was so diverted from the task at hand that I was not quieting my mind - I was listening to them breathing! It was distracting me trying to be quiet inside my own existence. Did quiet not mean quiet *breathing* too? I thought to myself that I needed to go deeper and block them out while just clearing my mind. My deep desire to inject some mechanics into my mediumship kept my mind moving forward with the task. Then, something really amazing happened. My mind let go and I was thrust into a massive room full of golden light. This room looked very ancient and it had an oriental look and feel to it. There were golden raw wooden columns holding up golden wooden beams in the ceiling. The wooden floor was golden too and it was like I was watching all of this happen through someone else's eyes. It was as though my consciousness had joined with another to allow me the vision I was experiencing. It was like I was in an ancient oriental temple but there was no feel of 'time'. Not time as you and I are aware of which slowly rolls by whether we are timing it or not. Time just seemed to stand still; it was suspended as I was just there in my consciousness as a witness to events in another dimension. I was in a moment of just 'being'. I became aware that I was looking through someone else's eyes who were sitting in that golden glowing room and *they* were meditating! From that vantage point I looked down and was aware of my golden glowing bare male chest – very smooth and muscular – rising and falling as breaths were deeply, quietly, inhaled then exhaled. I could see their legs crossed in meditation style and I felt very much at peace. I was taking all of this in and very much amazed at how I was watching all of this happen and wondering, even hoping, for something even more spectacular to occur which I could witness and tell the others about! It was just then that the leader called our attention back into the room. I found it hard to believe so much time had passed and that we were already pretty much finished! I looked around at the others to see if anyone else might have an expression of wonder or amazement on their face. Everyone just seemed to look at the floor or away when I glanced in their direction. Surely I was not the only one who saw this!

The leader sat with us for a moment to bring our awareness back into the current moment and then said he was going to his office so if anyone wanted to speak with him about their experience that they were welcome to come and speak with him one by one. A lady next to me jumped right up before I could even make a slight movement in his direction so I waited to go next.

I sat there for an eternity waiting my turn – my perception of time passing had returned if only for me to distort it once again. Finally my turn came and I was a little apprehensive about telling my friend's dad what had happened. But, that's why I was there and so I found some courage and went into his office. I sat down in front of this compassionate looking older gentleman and proceeded to tell him my tale.

With each sentence he became more engrossed in my story and at one point he asked me, "Did the man have a beard? A long white beard?"

I quickly searched my memory but could not recall seeing a long white beard across my smooth muscular chest so I had to say, "No, no beard." He seemed a little disappointed.

I finished telling about my experience and the teacher explained to me that part of what he did to prepare the room for meditation class was to connect with an ancient energy and charge the room with it. And then he said something I had not been expecting.

"You have tapped right into the energy I charged the room with. No one has ever done that before. I think you are too advanced for us and it's probably better if you don't come back again to class."

I just looked at him a little confused and I guess he sensed my questioning look. Then he continued, "You are too advanced for this class and you will more than likely get bored and not come back after a while. That will affect the balance of the class so it's best you don't come back again."

I didn't know what else to do so I thanked him and I left. I drove home with mixed emotions. On one hand I had just had the most amazing vision, which he had confirmed I might add, and on the other hand I had just been kicked out of a meditation class for being too advanced. I wish either he or I would have had the presence of mind to organize me into a class that fit me better. But, we didn't and there's really no point crying over it all these years later.

I finally arrived back home and my husband, Ajaz, asked me how it had all went. Since Ajaz had actually encouraged me to go to a meditation class in the first place he seemed really anxious to hear all about how I had found the experience. I just smiled and told him, "They asked me not to come back." You should have seen the look on his face! I'm not totally sure what all went through his mind but then I went on to explain all that had happened and he was very supportive of me – as usual. Ajaz hugged me tight and whispered encouragingly, "You'll find your place in the world someday." Funny, he's always right.

"Life is a quarry, out of which we are to mold and chisel a complete character."

—Samuel Butler
(1835 – 1902)
English Novelist

3. Open Circle

Organizing the house for my early evening departure can be quite a little fiasco. Tuesday night, 7:30 p.m. If the meeting were any earlier it would be impossible to attend. Any later and I would have collapsed in a heap of exhaustion for I had not had a full night's sleep for several years. Our daughter, Xara, had been awake every two hours for the first fourteen months of her life. She was two and a half years old when the twins, Rocco and Marcus, came along. Oh, bliss. So the extent of my exhaustion cannot be fully explained to the uninitiated. It too, is something that must be lived to be fully and completely appreciated.

My search for truth had taken me from my fourteen year old son, P.J., about 7 years earlier. I blindly followed my heart ignoring all others feelings. Something was driving me forward and I had no control over it. My Parents had already lost one child and I was to follow. The only exception being that one was lost *to* the grave and the other was seeking what was *beyond* it.

As I finished up the housework and handed the children off to my husband who had made a special effort to leave work early so I might have even the slightest chance of making the meeting on time; I peeled the last screaming child from my leg as I tried to brush off those heartbreaking comments that only a child can hurl, "Mummy don't leave me!" And then the eventual tear jerker – "But, I LOVE YOU Mummy." Sniff, sniff.

With my child resistant barrier neatly in place I made my way to the open door. I felt as though I had a date with destiny. The meeting started in 15 minutes and I had reconned the church which fit into my husband's schedule - all was in motion. I had to leave – now. Surely the church had sent a secret agent to Xara's nursery earlier that day in an effort to indoctrinate her against my eventual participation in their events. I pushed my way through the line of children blocking my advancement. Only one runny nose left and I closed the door behind me. I could, however, hear the barrage of insults being hurled from behind the closed door in a last ditch effort to subdue me. I resisted and drove out of the gates, mentally arming myself for my arrival at the meeting which was a fifteen minute journey away. There was no stopping me now, or so I thought. With every moment my anticipation rose!

As you can imagine I hit every red light that could possibly turn red for the whole length of England. Where was my sign from heaven that I was headed in the right direction - spiritually speaking? I had read all the books. Everyone else's journey went so smoothly. They had loads of road signs pointing the way. Where were all these so-called 'Guides' of mine? Then it occurred to me, my Guides must be trying to tell me something! Red lights? Go home. My mind shouted "NO!" I've come this far and now it was a battle of wills. And then I decided to try something I had read about in one of my books. I asked for help. "Please help me get to church on time." To my utter amazement all the lights for blocks and blocks began to change a lovely shade of green all at the same time. The cars ahead of me began to move swiftly and then turn down side streets as if they instinctively knew I really needed to get past them. It was like Moses had parted my sea of traffic.

Finally reaching the pre-arranged meeting I had a mixture of joy and trepidation. I had finally found a place I could come and meet other people "like me" and I could develop my gift and use it to help other people. (Funny how I always thought of helping others – wonder why I never thought of helping myself? This too I was to find out later on my journey.) So, I walked in and was happy to see other smiling faces that apparently seemed rather nonchalant about me turning up! My level of expectation was certainly much higher than what I perceived coming from others. I could not wait for the evening demonstration to begin. I wanted to watch the professional medium up on stage and wait for my turn at the end, during open circle, to show I was indeed worthy of being *allowed* into a development group. Up to that point in my short life I had tried very hard to not let people find out about my gift for fear of being ridiculed or perhaps that my children would be thought of as "the children of that strange woman" but, here I was and ready for the action to begin! You see, when I had first approached the church asking to join a development group I had been told, "It doesn't work that way. You will have to come to open circle for about six months and give messages to the audience. If you make a commitment and continue to come to church then we will see how it goes and then you might be invited to join a development group."

Once again, I had gone looking for guidance and direction only to be shot down. I was at least happy I had not been told to *not come back!*

So, I was ready and anxious for the proceedings to begin. First the proceedings began with a prayer and then there was singing of church type hymns. The visiting Medium was introduced without much fan fair and we were off! The demonstration lasted for about two hours and then it was time for the open circle portion of the meeting. This portion of the meeting was when developing Mediums, like me, who were in the audience, would stand up and give any messages they had received to others in the audience. I wondered how I could possibly get up and give any sort of a message even close to being as worthy as the messages the Medium had given for this collection of very willing participants!

I can remember the first time I stood up and gave someone in the audience a message. I will have to add at this point that I have terrible stage fright! Not normal stage fright that just makes you a little nervous when you have to speak in front of a crowd. No, I've got industrial strength stage fright – the kind that makes you want to hurl from across the room or go dig a hole and hide so no one can see you. The thought of making me stand up in front of a room of people, even today, makes me break out in a cold sweat! So I waited, and watched, as a few other people got up and gave their messages to the audience. I was watching what format I should use as I had never seen this done before.

After watching what was apparently the last willing medium give their message I realized it was my turn now! So I raised my hand to indicate that I too had a message and I was directed to 'stand and deliver'. The message I had received was for the woman sitting at the end of my row. I had watched an elderly man standing next to her – in spirit – smiling - during the whole evening. He had been quietly observing the proceedings – smoking a pipe and he had a feeling of celebration about him. Don't ask me how I knew this – I just knew. It's kind of like when your grandparents have that special – going out – outfit the wear all the time. It's kept put away until someone comes to fetch them and take them to some special family event. It's the outfit they think they look the best in or perhaps they've had the most compliments when they've worn it to outings. Well, that's what this gentleman was wearing – his special-occasion-going-out-outfit. And that is exactly what I told the woman at the end of my row. She slowly smiled in recognition and wiped away a tear while she nodded her head in agreement. Indeed, she knew him. It was her Dad and today was his birthday. She always took him out on his birthday as he grew older and she said that if he had still been alive she would have taken him out today too. She was very happy to hear from her Dad and was glad he had made their birthday outing even if she had not been aware of it – until now.

Then on to the man who was sitting a few rows directly in

front of me. I stood out in the aisle at this point and asked this nice looking man if I could speak with him for a moment? He smiled and looked a little uneasy and grinned at the lady sitting next to him as if he needed her approval first. I assumed it was his wife they way they had this little silent communication system going. I asked if I could talk to him and he sort of quickly ran it past her to see if it was okay with a questioning smile and a shake of his head – a slight shrug of his shoulders in agreement. I wondered how many times in life this man had to get this lady's approval but it seemed to work for them so I waited silently. She smiled back at him and put a reassuring hand on his shoulder. I suppose this subliminally steadied him or perhaps she was hoping I would pick up on her energy and read for her too? I wasn't really sure but just pushed on with this naughty little boy stood next to me in spirit waiting to talk to this uneasy big man.

I gave him this message, "I have a little boy here who has gotten my attention by coming directly at my head with a cricket bat as though he was going to hit me right in the face with it. I don't know if this is really your son but he gives me the feeling that you were sort of a father to him." I looked at the man who seemed a bit surprised and said, "No…..it's….not my son." He looked back at the woman to just check and make sure he was saying the right thing. I felt a little sorry for him to be so unsure of everything and his need to get this lady's input on matters I was sure he had full knowledge of. Surely he would know if he had a son in spirit or not but he felt compelled to just check with his missus to make sure he was correct. Maybe he was just checking to make sure he had heard me right? She smiled reassuringly at him and we carried on.

I said, "Well this boy does not want to talk to me about the way he passed. It seems that he was a naughty little boy quite a lot of the time and it may have been something to do with being naughty that caused him to pass." I kept looking at the man in front of me who had become very still and stared straight ahead and then dipped his head toward the floor as he bent over resting his forearms on his legs, studying my every word, with his hands clasped in front of him.

I continued, "I see a lot of sports equipment around him. Not just cricket bats but baseball equipment and basketballs – all kinds of sports here. He's still giving me this feeling that you were the only father figure he ever knew even if he was not your son. You were like a dad to him. He wants to thank you for that and tell you that you *do* make a difference. That's all he wants to tell you. He wants you to know that you *do* make a difference and that you made a difference in his life at one time."

I stood there as the man looked shocked at his wife again and began to stammer as he explained something very important to me and everyone else sitting in the room. He looked back at me and said, "Well....you see....he's not my son. My son is alive.....but, I don't know who this might be.....but, well....you see....I've been involved with the Big Brother's Organization for about 20 years and I've known lots of little boys...and....well.... I was just telling my wife that I was going to stop going because I didn't feel like I made any difference to anyone there. I....I guess maybe I did....I do."

Then this nice man wiped a tear from his eye and just stared at the ground. He looked a bit choked up and didn't want to look up again. I guess he felt a bit humbled too. His wife patted her hand on his shoulder as a very proud smile beamed from her and, she too, wiped a tear that streamed down her cheek. It took a naughty little boy who had passed over to let this giant of a man know what good work he had been doing and that he should keep it up because he was making a difference in other little boys lives too. This spirit standing there could have told me his name or something that the man could have recognized but that's not what was important to him. What was important was conveyed that night. That was all that mattered really. Spirit is watching us in our daily lives and they know about the troubles we go through. They understand when we are feeling low or sometimes when we just need to feel a bit appreciated. I'm glad I had the courage to stand up in front of this crowd of people to give a little message to this man. This very small message had touched this man's heart and I'm sure it made a big difference in some decisions he made in his life going forward. It's actually a good message for all of us. We don't always know how our little acts of kindness affect others immediately. Sometimes it takes a while to find out and sometimes we never know how we've influenced others. Just keep doing the best you can. Give a smile, a hug, share a laugh. It all gets counted in the end. Do the best you can and God will give you credit for the rest. He's a pretty smart guy.

And so, I carried on going to Open Circle week after week and giving readings at the end of the demonstration to the congregation. This one story really sticks with me because on this particular day my mother went with me to the demonstration. Mom didn't normally go with me as they live in the USA but they were in the UK on a visit so Mom came along with me that evening. We went into the church, found some seats and soon it was time for the service to begin. The medium was on stage and had begun giving people from the audience messages. Mom was sitting next to me as I started receiving a message, not from the demonstrating medium but from spirit, for the woman sitting directly in front of me. I could see my Mom out of my peripheral vision as I watched, on this occasion, a story unreel on the back of the wooden folding chair directly in front of me.

The woman sitting in front of me had sat right on the very front row and on the very inside aisle seat in what I call an earnest effort to get a reading from the visiting medium. Oh yes, the visiting medium was well aware of this woman's deeply intense desire I can assure you. This woman on the front row, who wore a headscarf, was leaning in the direction of the medium every time she walked past. She was like a human magnet trying to attract the medium her way with her body language and sheer will. It was obvious the woman had probably had a treatment for cancer but, I am just guessing.

Perhaps some other condition, or stress, had caused her hair to fall out and that's why she wore the headscarf.

During most of the demonstration I had a scene develop on the back of this woman's wooden folding chair and I sat staring at it intently. It was like a cartoon come to life but, it was far from funny. I watched the scenes appear and change and tried to keep track of all the messages coming from the images. When the images would stop I would try to hold on to what I had been shown as it would be nearly two hours until I got to give my message out and I didn't want to forget any of it. Often as I am going over the information the messages will start up again and I will have to add those new messages to the ones I am trying to not forget. It's much easier to just give a straight forward reading than it is to go through this process of holding on to a message for hours at a time before you can give it out. But, this is the process I had to go through in the beginning of my development. Sometimes I would find myself questioning what I was seeing or I would second guess my initial impression of what I was shown. I often thought it was a sort of mental conditioning exercise but I'm glad I don't have to go through that anymore.

Finally, the demonstrating medium drew to a finished on stage and it was time for Open Circle once again. As usual my stage fright kicked in and I waited for a few other people to give their messages first to see if anyone would go to this woman in front of me and let me off the hook! No one did – so when it was obvious I would have to give my message I went to the front. Yes, the dreaded front – in front of everyone – like I want to pass out 'cos they're all staring at me – very very front!! I had to go to the front so I could face this woman sitting on the very *front* row. So, I looked at this woman on the front row and ask her if I could come to her with a message? She looked back at me with the most hope filled eyes I have ever seen and I thought she would burst into tears right there. "Oh, yes please." My stage fright melted as I saw the hope and love beaming from this lady's eyes. I was not there to worry about people looking at me I was there to deliver a message from spirit to her and she instantly soothed my worried soul.

And so I began, "As I was sitting behind you I became aware of a scene from Dante's Inferno on the back of your chair. I don't know if Dante's Inferno means anything in particular to you (she shook her head no) but I will tell you that this is a representation of what it is like in Hell. (I did not tell her about the people writhing in pain – nor the screams of torment I witnessed because I have to interpret what I am seeing – If I were to tell her this she might think *she* was going to hell which is certainly not what the message was about) So I explained it this way, "To me, this is telling me that you have been going through your own version of a hell-type situation." (She shook her head in agreement this time and brought her hands up in front of her in gentle prayer position as she seemed to hold her breath waiting for more information to come) "I want you to know that all of your prayers have been heard." And then Spirit began showing me another scene as I stood there trying to remember everything I had already been shown over the last two hours! "What Spirit are showing me is lots and lots of books open in front of you – this has been a learning experience for you and they are showing me that you will be going on to do some more learning – and courses - and that you are going to use all of this knowledge to help other people. You will be taking everything you have been learning and moving forward with it in a positive way to help other people. You have been given these experiences so you can truly relate to others and the experiences you have gone through, and are now going through, could not have been learned in books."

She raised her hands again as they had started to slowly slip down as she was listening, still in prayer position, and pressed them to her lips then lowered them to her lap. She seemed dazed and was quiet. I too was quiet and waiting for either more information from Spirit or perhaps giving this lady a chance to respond if she wanted to. The audience was quiet too and then this woman found her voice. I guess she could feel it in the air that everyone was curious if she had a response or not. From the time I finished speaking until she found her voice really wasn't that long at all. It was just the tension in the air that made it feel like time had stopped completely.

She looked up and smiled such a big smile and said, "I came here tonight… and I had begged (spirit) to please get me a reading. I asked God to please give me a message. I….I just needed some hope. Thank you so..so….. much." Then she reached over and hugged me. I could feel her whole body trembling as she squeezed me tight and then slowly released me with another glorious smile.

I went back to my seat and looked at Mom. She sat there with tears streaming down her red face and wiping them desperately with a limp exhausted tissue. I was confused. Mom was really crying and sniffing – and wiping! She whispered to me, "This must be a curse you have lived with all these years - to see such things – it's a curse. But, that lady got something good out of it. Some things are hard to understand." I just smiled, nodded and gave Mom a little hug. There were no more people either willing or able to get up and give anymore readings to the congregation so the service was finished off and we all gave our thanks to the visiting medium for their wonderful efforts for the evening.

When the last prayer was finished and the service was over we walked out, went home and had tea and biscuits. It was time for bed and a little rest. I did silently hope I had given that lady some comfort. If nothing else in life we all deserve that. She deserved to know she wasn't walking her journey alone. She deserved to know that her faith was able to carry her through the darkest of days and that the Angels are never absent from our presence often carrying us when we no longer have the strength to go even one more step on our own. We are precious beings of light who often forget who we are and why we are here. Our journey often takes us on perilous paths but we have the grace of God to shine brightly and show us the way back home.

I realized I didn't have to hide my gift any longer. I didn't have to study alone if I didn't want to. There are other people out in the world with the same gifts as me and there are also people out there in the world who want to hear what we can tell them even if it is just one small message that means the world – to them.

There are just a couple more stories I want to share with you before we push on. I have so much to tell you I often want to jump ahead of myself but I will try to stay calm and do this in an orderly fashion.

I used to stay home on the day of open circle and relax so I could really be ready for the evening meeting. I wanted to be open and receptive to what was becoming more meaningful communications. I was at home that day and in my kitchen doing a little of this and a little of that when a gentleman in spirit came walking into the kitchen from the open hallway door. (Spirit does seem to like my kitchen or maybe that's just where I spend a lot of time!) He didn't say anything to me he just came walking in – paced past me with his face looking down at the floor as though he was really thinking about something important and then he walked out the door to the hall again. I took this to be him impatiently pacing back and forth and probably a character trait he had when he was still alive in his physical body. He was obviously waiting for the evening's events too. This had happened before where I had spirit show up several hours before a meeting just to 'hang around'. As it normally turned out they either had friends or family show up whom I could place them with and they could give some sort of message to them. Well, this chap was 'jumping the queue' or should I say he was 'cutting in line' as he surely had a message to get to someone later that evening and he didn't want to wait on me making the connection later that evening. He wanted to be sure I was aware of him in plenty of time to make a connection. As he paced in and out of the kitchen I could plainly see what he was wearing. I knew for sure someone would be able to place him by his red suspenders and what looked like a red sort of lumberjack shirt and tan trousers. He was a stocky man in about his 60's and very active but he wasn't ready to 'talk' to me he just wanted to hang around until he could 'talk' to someone at the meeting. So when it was time for me to go to my weekly meeting I was sure this chap had gone ahead to make arrangements so I had a good seat.

Arriving at the meeting I could see that it would be a full house that night. I found a lone seat near the wall toward the back on the left. It was as if someone had saved that one seat for me! Tell me, who goes into an aisle and doesn't sit in the last seat against the wall? Why leave one seat open? I just thought it was curious. The service started and after prayers and the singing of hymns the visiting Medium began giving readings to a very receptive audience. As the evening got to about half way through the proceedings I had the man who was in my kitchen earlier that day show up again. He was standing way off to the right side near the far wall behind two ladies. Yep! I had clear and plain sight of who he wanted to speak with. He just smiled at me; gave me a thumbs up sign and waited.

When the time came for open circle I always wanted to let anyone else who had a message go first. It had just become a habit for me. Somehow tonight was different though. This man was ready and I was too so I got right up to give my message. Well, to give *his* message. I asked the two ladies if I could come to them and of course they were happy to talk to me. Our conversation went something like this, "I have an older gentleman here with me – actually he's standing between the two of you so I assume you two must be important to him. He stands between you and not off to just one of your sides." I watched the two ladies just smile and wait for more information. "I have to tell you that this man came to my house today and was milling in and out of the kitchen. In and out, in and out, just milling – pacing back and forth – very impatient for this evening to get here so he could speak to you. I believe this is how he was when he was alive. A bit impatient and he liked to pace and think." I motioned my hand to demonstrate him going in and out of the kitchen. One lady seemed to recognize this behavior and laughed while shaking her head in agreement. I was pleased she could accept this man after all the effort he had made to connect with her.

I then told the ladies how the gentleman standing behind them was dressed and the woman closer to me, the older woman, broadly smiled in recognition of his casual outfit. She shook her head in agreement and a resounding; "Yes." was shared with all of us encouraging more to be added to the message.

I continued, "He is giving me the feeling that he is a jack of all trades. He's stressing he's a JACK of all trades." Again she was shaking her head in agreement and added, "That's his name - JACK!" I was very pleased she knew who this man was but I smiled and quickly asked her to not tell me anything as I wanted to share with her what *he* was telling *me*. She smiled and shook her head in agreement and I carried on.

"I have just asked Jack what he did for a living when he was here (in the physical) and he quickly shows me a brick wall he is working on. He's got a trowel and cement and he's building a brick wall. He's very precise and very meticulous in his building methods. He was a bricky." (Bricky is the British word for someone who lays bricks for a living.) The lady smiled and said, "That's right."

"Now, I've been told in the past that you shouldn't go to someone unless you have a message for them but, I cannot tell what Jack's message is. He came to my house this afternoon to make sure I was aware of him. Then he shows me what he's wearing and what his name is and what his job was but I don't seem to be getting any particular message from him. He just keeps smiling at me and giving me the thumbs up sign." I cocked my head sideways at the lady and stuck my thumb up demonstrating what Jack was doing standing next to her.

The lady was really smiling by that time and rather loudly said, "That's Jack! If I ever asked him a question about anything he wouldn't give me a straight answer. He would just give me a thumbs up or a thumbs down sign. I have been asking him if I'm making the right decision about something very important and I was hoping he would be here tonight and tell me. That's all I needed to know! I know that's Jack. Thank you!"

So, once again, it wasn't important if I understood the message or not. All that was important is that this lady knew who was speaking to her from the spirit world and that *she* understood the message. All that was important is that I was there and able to understand enough of what Jack wanted to say and then I was able to relay that message to his waiting family. I am always so honored after every meeting when I have had the opportunity to be of service. Message received and understood. But, of course, this is one of the things I was taught in development class – never add or take away from the message you are being given from spirit. *They* know exactly what they want to say and *exactly* how to say it in a way that will be understood. If I had changed it in any way the message may not have had the same meaning to these jolly little ladies.

And finally, I think the hardest reading I ever gave at open circle was to a lady who just refused to communicate with me. The only time she did answer me was when I asked her if I could come to her with a message. She enthusiastically said, "YES." And that was pretty much the last sound she made. While I fully agree that the audience shouldn't 'feed' the medium information we still need direction while we are giving the reading as this helps us know which direction to go sometimes if there isn't a lot of information to go on when we first connect with someone in spirit. Getting a little feedback helps to build the intensity of the message. This lady must have been of the opinion that she was going to make me work for it. And so I did. To begin with the lady refused to look at me as though she thought maybe I was reading her mind instead of listening to Spirit. I really don't know what drives some people to look for a reading when they are so afraid of what they might hear or if they are so sure it's all just one big scam or something.

I carried on, "I have a lady here with me who shows me she was quite old when she passed. This older lady is wearing a long white sort of fantasia dress and she isn't wearing any shoes. She was very much a sort of hippie and she believed in 'all this stuff'." I motioned my hand around in a circle implying that the woman believed in spiritual things and particularly in mediumship. The whole time I was speaking to the woman seated in the audience she would hardly look at me. It was as if she was blocking me totally and it really had me quite confused and a little bit annoyed. At one point I wondered if I should just walk off and leave her sitting there as I felt she was being rather ignorant toward me.

I asked the woman, "Do you know this woman I am describing to you?"

She briefly looked at me and just said one sharp word, "No."

Well, this did throw me. I looked at the woman seated next to her wondering if I had come to the wrong woman. But, the woman in Spirit carried on giving me more information so I continued relaying that message.

"This woman is showing me that she died with a condition in her throat. I can feel this woman was a very heavy smoker which eventually led to throat cancer. Do you know who this is now that I'm speaking about?"

She just made a scrunched up nose and squinted eyes at me like a confused child does – shook her head and again said, "No."

I quickly glanced around to see if there was anyone trying to get my attention – perhaps someone who did know who this woman was and *wanted* to receive this message. No takers and I was sure I was with the right lady so I made one more attempt to get a message through to her.

"This lady wants to let you know that she is aware of a certain gentleman you are having problems with and she doesn't want you making the same mistakes over again like she did. Can you understand what she's talking about?"

Well three times certainly isn't a charm because this lady was looking at me like I was from another planet. Again she answered in the negative and I thanked her and went back to my seat feeling like a total idiot. I could see this woman in spirit clearly and had specific details about her and yet this woman refused to acknowledge her or the message she was bringing.

We finished up the meeting and I noticed the woman I had been speaking to earlier about the hippie type woman with throat cancer pop right up out of her chair and make a very hasty exit. I thought that was very strange indeed. I wondered if she thought I would try to confront her to clarify anything or if she was just so afraid that she wanted to get straight out of there. It was nothing to me if she didn't want to listen or if she couldn't remember who this lady in spirit was. This lady in spirit thought it was important enough for me to carry on trying to get through to her even if she didn't want to hear it.

I decided it was time for me to go home early so I passed on having tea and biscuits with post meeting guests. I felt a little confused and my ego had been a little bruised with this lady's earlier behavior. I got my coat on and walked past everyone in the line for tea as I said my good-byes to everyone and made my way out the door to the street. You will never believe what I witnessed there in this side street. The woman who had completely refused to listen to the spirit and her advice had taken out her mobile phone and was excitedly talking to someone on the other end. She was so involved in her conversation that she didn't even notice me standing on the sidewalk stunned. "I can't believe what she told me! She described her exactly to me! Can you believe it? I just can't believe it and she even knew about her cancer! Can you believe it? And you will never believe what she told me next! That I should get rid of the man I'm having problems with and not end up like her!! OH MY GOD! Can you believe she said that?! It's just so amazing!!"

And then she looked up and saw me standing just outside the door of the church and smiled at me. This woman who earlier would not acknowledge me or the spirit who was trying to communicate with her was obviously blown away by the message she had been given. She was so absorbed in her mobile phone conversation that she was standing in the middle of the road ranting to someone about what she had just been told. I was glad I had walked up on her conversation as I was really confused about what had gone wrong with the reading I was offering to bring through for spirit.

I supposed this may have been her mother in spirit and, just like in real life; sometimes we don't want to listen to our parents. Perhaps she had behaved toward me with the same defiant demeanor she had toward her mother when she was alive. I just had to guess but at least I went home feeling a bit lighter when I saw the rest of the story unfolding out on the side street to a very excited woman sharing her message with someone on the telephone. I learned a really good lesson that night. But, gosh it was hard! Spirit has never lied to me. I set up some rules in the beginning of my development that I stick hard and fast to. I only accept the truth and I only talk to those of God's light. It's been a couple of really good rules to have.

"There is nothing to fear except the persistent refusal to find out the truth, thepersistent refusal to analyze the causes of happenings."

—Dorothy Thompson
(1893 – 1961)
American Journalist

4. An Important Message (for me)

I have spent many years feeling very annoyed with myself and I will tell you why. Although I have tried very hard to learn all I could spiritually in an effort to decipher the messages I receive I have found that, at times, I am unable to learn the value of the message until after the event has passed. No matter how hard I try...I can meditate, I can ask my Guides, I can plead to the twinkling stars and watch for some clue – even hoping just for a shooting star to confirm there is someone out there listening to my plight. But no answer apparently comes. Of course I'm not talking about when I'm getting information for others – it's getting information for me that I find so difficult.

I have spent many years searching and not finding or so I thought at the time. I have wondered if I am just very ignorant or perhaps the answer is presented and I am just so busy with the rest of my very hectic life and children that I totally missed that shining moment of truth. I have wondered what beacons of light have been lobbed against my very thick head and just bounced off unnoticed?

And then one weekend I attended an event at the Gorton Monastery near Manchester, UK. I believe it was officially 'Angel Day' or something like that. The Gorton Monastery is an absolutely beautiful building full of history and magic which still permeates even the blades of grass which rise up from the gently manicured gardens. I was introduced to a 'friend of a friend' like happens so often at this sort of event; a lovely lady named Angela. My friend, Ladan, was working her own stall and Angela and I went off to sit in the garden for just a bit during the break in the program. We chatted very briefly about spiritual 'this and that' and I mentioned how I had often wondered why it was that I seemed to be pretty good at getting messages for other people, say, at demonstrations of mediumship but, at other times I had premonitions that I was totally unable to decipher.

With her shining inquisitive eyes she quipped, "May I come into your space and try to find out for you?" Without trying to sound too wildly eager I merely answered, "Yes, please."

Angela straightened herself up slightly as we were sitting on the grass under the shade of a lovely old tree. She folded her hands and I hoped to myself she could find out the answer to this question that has plagued me for so long.

After a few moments, (and yes, I was quite impressed at her speed!) she first asked if it was okay to give me a hug which I gladly accepted and returned. Part of her message to me was private and I do not feel I can share it just yet. But, the rest was absolutely music to my heart.

Angela told me that my mediumship is a by-product of the real reason I AM here. She told me some things I already knew so that's why the rest of what she said made so much sense to me. Angela has lifted a burden I have carried for many years.

I AM a Being of Light. Mainly, I AM here to bring others to the Light. It is because of that connection to the Light that I AM able to perceive other dimensions and the Light Beings which are there, or should I say – here? It just made so much sense to me, finally. Some of the things I sense, see, hear and just know aren't meant for me to decipher. It's a part of my reality just like the sun shining or a bird flying past an open window. I can see it – so I do. There is no other reason for it.

Some will say that if I have this gift I should try to develop it and help people. Well, I try to help everyone I can. I was not sent here to save the world. I was sent here to be a sort of crossing guard. You must check the road before you cross. Use your common sense and then stop and look both ways before making those big decisions. Don't wait for me to tell you its all clear. I may not see exactly what you see coming down the street but, I will try to stop the traffic if you stumble in the middle of the road or walk just a little bit too slowly in the busy streets. Other than that it's pretty much up to you how fast you go and in what direction you choose. Educating oneself is the biggest responsibility there is.

Thank you, Angela. You really were *my* Angel that day! I guess Spirit thought I had suffered enough with that big weight on my shoulders. And it wasn't even my birthday!

"Having somewhere to go is what we call home. Having someone to love, who loves us in return, is what we call family. Having both; a blessing."

—Donna Hedges

5. Baby Monitor

I was waked at 2:00 a.m. by the sound of laughing on the baby monitor that lived in the twin's room on top of a chest of drawers. Marcus was awake and chattering to someone. But, I could not hear Rocco chattering back to him. It was quite a one sided conversation he had going on and it was filled with laughter too. I thought perhaps I should go down the hall and have a quick look at what this little man was up to. The boys were about eighteen months old at this point and I was still struggling to get a full night's sleep. This sounded like it needed to be investigated though so I drug myself up and walked quietly down the hall hoping this wouldn't take too long to resolve.

As I slowly opened the door to their bedroom the light from the hall illuminated a portion of their darkened room. I could see that Marcus was standing at the end of his baby bed holding on to the footboard part. Both of his little hands grasped on tight and he was ducking behind the solid wooden footboard and then sticking his head back up as if playing peek-a-boo with someone whom I could not see. In between his head bobbing up and down there where those lovely baby giggles and broad smiles with each raised head. Marcus had noticed me standing there but was just too engrossed in his game to pay me any attention. So, I asked him, "Are you playing with Grandma?" (This particular week was the one year anniversary of the passing of my mother-in law, Balquees.) Marcus stopped what he was doing and backed himself up to about the middle of his bed. He was steadying himself in his little all-in-one nighty with both hands holding on to the opposite sides of the crib. He was listening to me but he was still listening to someone else too. I was trying very hard to see/hear/feel – whatever possible as I wanted to know who was in my little lad's bedroom at 2 a.m.! It all happened so fast that I didn't really have time to organize a plan as to how to proceed. I just went with the flow as I have done so many times in the past. When these things happen it's best to stay calm and not get too freaked out!

I asked him again who he was playing with and he turned his head toward the end of the bed once more and then he turned his whole head – tracking someone as he watched this invisible visitor move all the way around the end of his bed and continue all the way around his sleeping brothers bed then up to the top of Rocco's bed near the wall. It was amazing to watch this happening in front of me! Marcus turned and looked at me as I asked him once again who he was playing with. Part of my questioning Marcus was to merely acknowledge the presence of Spirit and part of it was to reassure Marcus that everything was okay – not that he really needed it! Then he turned his head all the way around to look back to the other side of the room and extended one arm up as if to point at whomever he was playing with. It was like he was saying, "Look there Mom – over there, see?" Marcus then watched Spirit walk all the way back around both beds and when they reached what would have been the end of his footboard Marcus squealed with laughter again. Well, I was at least happy about that but his sheer squeal was a little unsettling to me if I'm honest. I was wide awake now! I had a quick look and Rocco was still sound asleep in the neighboring bed.

I thought the event had ended as Marcus reached up for me to take him out of his baby bed. But, I was wrong. He only wanted me to take him out so he could get down on the floor. The moment he got on the floor he started to play another game with our invisible friend! You know the game – the 'here I come, I'm going to get you and tickle you' game. Marcus would go towards the far end of the room with his tickly fingers ready as if sneaking up on someone then he would turn and run squealing to me as if someone was just about to get him! This happened a few times and then I decided if I didn't do something that this would go on all night. Not having slept much myself for many months I also didn't want to encourage a nightly visitation either. Yes, mothers can be so selfish!

So, I got Marcus's attention and picked him back up. I told him that it was time for him to go back to sleep and put him back in his bed. He was standing in the middle of his bed and looking back toward the footboard where Spirit would have been standing to begin with. Marcus would look at me when I was talking to him and then he would turn his head and 'listen' to whatever Spirit was telling him too as soon as I would stop talking. I told Marcus that it was time to go to sleep now and that he could play with 'Grandma' tomorrow. He took one long last look at the end of the bed as if listening to someone say goodnight. He then flopped himself down on the bed, inserted pacifier in his mouth, closed his eyes and went to sleep as if I had turned his switch off! I stood for a moment in the quiet room to try to sense who or what we had just witnessed. I sent out my prayers of protection for my children and I asked that the identity of the Spirit visitor be made known to me - if not now then at sometime in the future. A couple of weeks later I was amazed when I got my answer.

I was at my spiritual development class. (Did I mention that I finally got accepted into a class? Well, I did and it didn't take six months of evaluations before I was invited either.)

The class went as normal, which is to say we would meditate and pick up any messages for each other and then we would share our experiences at the end of the evening. When it came time to express our experiences for that particular evening we, or should I say I, had a surprise. One gentleman (I will call him Tom) who admitted to very rarely having 'spirit' communications wanted to pass on a message to *me*. He said this spirit came through very clearly and you could see that Tom was still somewhat surprised by the whole experience too. Tom had the spirit of my son with him and this is what he said to me,

"Well, Michelle, I have this lad here who seems to me to be about 19 or 20 years old which doesn't seem right to me because I know your children are very small. (My twins were 18 months and Xara was 4 years old) And, he tells me that you are his mother and he even puts his arm around your shoulders and says for me to tell you that he loves you very much. He is very tall – taller than you. He just wants me to tell you how much he loves you and that you need to know *it was him*. You must have asked this question about something that happened and he just says to tell you that- it was him. I'm sorry Michelle this doesn't seem to make much sense to me but I hope you can take it."

Well, YES I can take it! What joy to have this message. My son who had died as a baby had just given a very important message to my friend who barely knew me. And the connections were astounding to me. Remember I said that at the time of Marcus having his playful visitor in his room that it was the one year passing of Balquees, my mother-in-law? Well, it was also the week that my second born son, who was also named Marcus, would have been 20. It was his birthday and he came to have a play with his little brother who was also his namesake! And even more astounding was that he had given the message to someone in my group who admits to not receiving messages from Spirit and knew nothing about my older children.

I learned a very important lesson that night at development class. I learned that when you ask for help it will always be given. If you try to work with spirit then they will always try to work with you too.

"For He shall give his angels charge over thee to keep thee in all thy ways."

The Bible
—Psalms 91:11

6. Angel Ice Cream

Sometimes children can seem so wise beyond their years. Perhaps it's because they have access to a world which has pretty much been erased from the memories of adults. Children are born with the same natural gift that we were all born with. I can remember myself as a small child. I was so afraid to go to bed at night like a lot of children are. That was the time when the world was quiet and the room was pitch black, when I could see and hear spirit the clearest. I was sure that if I kept my covers pulled up tight that I would be okay – maybe they wouldn't see me!

My clearest recollection late one night is of a woman running down our hall screaming. I was terrified! What was she running from and more importantly why was she screaming? I only experienced her that one time and now as an adult I know that it was a lost spirit in our house that night. I believe we have all had such experiences at different times of our lives. Sometimes you just don't want to admit what it is that you have experienced and sometimes it's not important to your journey this time anyway. So you just go on with your 'reality' portion of your programming and leave the spirit world to anyone else who is brave enough to venture into the subject.

My best memory as a child was one stormy night. Yes, I

know that sounds a strange way to start a good memory but just hang on with me for a moment. My bedroom was in one corner of the house and the moon shining on trees swaying outside made scary looking shadows on the windows and in the room. So, this one stormy night I was really scared all by myself in my dark room. I always had the covers over my head because I knew if I held my breath and stayed covered up then I would actually be invisible. Well, that was my reasoning then but I guess all that lack of oxygen as a child could well explain a lot about me now! When we were little there were no nightlights and we were growing up in the "conserve energy" era so there were certainly no lights left on in the closet or bathroom to cast a little light down the hall or into my room.

The storm was raging outside and there was terrible lightening and hard driving rain. The weather can really be harsh and unpredictable in southern Texas. With every lightening strike my fear seemed to grow and I even lowered the covers at one point to make sure I was still alone in the room – that's when something caught my attention. After the lightening strike had diminished there was still a soft glow in the room. I was too young to wonder if my eyesight was malfunctioning although that would be my first conclusion now days. No, instead of throwing the covers back up over my head to resume invisibility I continued to look at that warm gentle glow in the room. The glow built and I can only say to you now that it was an Angel. I was not afraid. This Angel came closer and as it extended its arm toward me an ice cream cone appeared (in my inner vision). It was one of those brown sugar cones with the pointy bottom and a lovely round scoop of ice cream on the top. Now this was a treat as we were not really allowed sweets when we were children. I remember as I went to have a lick of the ice cream an overwhelming sense of peace and well-being came over me and I fell into a deep sleep. After that I was never quite so afraid at night any longer and I look at each ice cream cone with a fond sense of remembering.

"Dreams are today's answers to tomorrow's questions."

—Edgar Cayce
American Psychic/Clairvoyant
(1877 – 1945)

7. Deathly Premonitions (and goodbyes)

When I was growing up I became aware that I often had dreams that came true. It happened all the time and it was sort of funny to tell my family things – then it would happen - then they would say, "Oh, guess what happened!" And then they would go on to explain that what I had dreamed about had actually come true. It was a load of little things and then one day my older brother, Mike, actually said jokingly to me that if I ever dreamed about him – he didn't want to know! After what happened next I understand why he said that.

I can't remember the exact date as back then I didn't write things down the way I do now. Back then it was all a bit of fun and sometimes it was a bit scary too. I had not told anyone that I could hear people talking when no one was there or that I could see spirit or that there were times I would wake up and I was not inside my body! They could hardly accept the fact that I had dreams that came true so do you really think I was ready to share with them the possibility that all this other stuff was happening too?So one night in early December 1989, I went to sleep and I had this terrible awful horrible dream that still sticks with me. In the dream it was pitch black and I had the feeling of my sister,

Michawn. It was her energy I was picking up on. I was tumbling over and over in the pitch black and I was filled with this sense of deep mourning. I was crying in the dream as though someone had died and it was my sister I was connecting to. I woke up out of the dream and I was sobbing. I was filled with the actual feeling that someone had died and could make no sense of this. At the time my sister was 16 years old and it did not make sense that I should connect this young person to anything other than happiness and life. I shook off the feeling of dread and went back to sleep. To my horror the dream started up again. You know – same feel – same theme. I was again filled with dread and a sense of deep mourning. I was again in this pitch black darkness and rolling over and over in the dark only this time I was connecting with the energy of my sister's boyfriend, Russ. Once again I woke up sobbing. Once again I was at a loss as to why I would have this terrible dream and now twice in the same night. The first dream with Michawn in it and the second time – exactly the same dream but, now featuring Russ. I was to find out two weeks later exactly what the dream meant.

December 16, 1989.

Michawn and Russ left a party and were making their way home on a very cold dark winter's night. It has been reported that it was the coldest night that we saw in that part of Texas for many years and it was very black that night. A flatbed 18-wheeler had tried to make a u-turn across a five lane highway just on the outskirts of town where there were not any streetlights. His truck had become disabled and the driver decided to abandon his truck and walk to a nearby truck stop to try to find some help. Unfortunately, he did not have the presence of mind to put out safety flares or cones or to even leave the lights of his truck on so that anyone else who might be traveling past could see and avoid him. Russ and Michawn's car struck the side of the flatbed trailer - head on - with fatal results. At that time the seatbelt law had not been in effect for very long and neither of them was wearing their seatbelts. They were not restrained in the car and that is probably the rolling or tumbling effect I had felt in the dream.

I used to feel very guilty that I had had that dream and then not known what to do with the information. Was Spirit trying to help me prevent this accident? That's a question I struggled with for many years but now I don't think so. I do think Spirit used a very powerful event in our lives to help me to wake up and pay attention. There was definitely something supernatural going on and this event completely changed my life. Not just because we had lost two very special people in our lives but because it was like Spirit shouting out to me that there really was more out there and they wanted to help me if I would just listen and work with them.

Russ died in the accident that night and Michawn was in a coma for three days before my parents had the heart wrenching decision to turn off her life support as the doctors delivered the news that she was, in fact, 'brain dead'. I think the doctors used such a graphic term in an effort to get my parents to be able to let go and allow Michawn's life to go on in others. The doctors had requested that Michawn be allowed to be an organ donor and it was the Christmas season so there was apparently a greater shortage than normal for donors. My parents agreed and I know it has been a decision they really did struggle with but, Michawn was a very loving, giving person and I'm sure she would have signed the paper herself if she had been able to.

My brother, Mike, lived with a self-imposed guilt that he could have prevented what happened that cold dark night in December if he had only driven them to the party. Michawn and Russ had invited Mike along to the party but, he was busy and declined. He silently carried the burden of that guilt with him until many years later when he came to visit me in England. Mike was quite interested to see what went on at an Open Circle meeting and so he came along with me one night. The visiting medium came to him and asked if she might speak with him for a moment. Of course, he agreed and we listened intently to what came next. The medium told Mike she had a young lady with her who she felt to be his sister. Next, the medium described Michawn down to a tee even listing the way she wore her hair with a slant cut in the front and half hanging across her face as well as having passed away from a car accident. She talked about seeing cheerleader's pom poms which was also true. Michawn had been on the drill team for our local high school and part of her equipment was pom poms used during their routines. We all sat there listening to each word this woman blessed us with – news from our sister in the spirit world. And then, without going into any great detail, the medium gave Mike the best news he ever heard. "She wants to tell you it's not your fault and you should stop blaming yourself for what happened. She loves you very much." There was more this woman had to say but it was hard to concentrate on her after that revelation. My poor brother had burst out crying and years of torment flowed from him in waves of relief. Once again, one small message spoke volumes to another person's heart. That one message changed Mike's life forever more. It really was a blessing for him that night.

Not long after Michawn and Russ' funerals I had another dream. This time it was just Russ in the dream. At the time I was working at a Walgreen's and in the dream I was standing on one aisle in particular stocking a shelf. I noticed someone come walking around the end of the aisle and as I paid more attention I realized it was Russ. Of course, I was surprised to see him but he was dressed in his normal clothes of a white T-Shirt and light blue long walking shorts kind of like the surfer shorts all the kids used to wear in the '80s. One thing I did notice was that he was not wearing any shoes. I also noticed that he had a big scar on the ankle of one foot.I said to him, "Russ, where have you been?"

And he said to me, "I Am where I Am." (That made no sense to me at the time.)

Just then we both began floating toward the ceiling and as we got to where the ceiling should have been we both floated right through it. We came up through the ceiling and we were in fluffy white mist and behind Russ was the most beautiful blue color I have ever seen. It just surrounded him - all this beautiful blue and I became upset as I knew he was in the spirit world and I yelled, "Russ!" and as I did my vision faded and I woke up. I don't know why I shouted out his name. Perhaps it's because we did not get to say goodbye to him. Due to the extent of Russ' injuries he needed to have a closed casket service. Perhaps this was Russ saying goodbye to me that night?

A short while after that dream I was able to tell Russ' Mother the dream I had had with Russ' visit. I told her about how he was dressed and that he had no shoes on. She looked really surprised when I told her about the big scar on Russ' foot and she said, "No one knew about that scar! Even though it was an old scar and had faded he still kept it hidden because he was so embarrassed by it. There is no way you could have known he had that scar." How amazing is that to get a confirmation directly from a close family member? Russ had made sure I saw that scar for a reason and now his Mom was confirming that it was not a dream – it was really Russ!

Next, my own mother was telling an aunt about the dream I had and when she told her the cryptic message, "I Am where I Am." Well, my bible thumping church going aunt (I say this with the utmost respect) could not believe her ears. This is a phrase from the bible although the phrase states, "I AM who I AM", it still refers to being with God. I suppose I may have heard this at church growing up but had not taken any notice of it before. It was an amazing vision and I have not had a single worry about where Russ is or what he may be doing since.

"Success does not consist in never making mistakes but in never making the same one a second time."

—George Bernard Shaw
(1856-1950)
Irish Playwright

8. America's Most Wanted

There were other things that happened back in my 20's that made everyone sort of stop and think from time to time. My brother, Mike, had a professional band. For awhile it was a rock-n-roll band and then it naturally turned into a country band. Well, we were in Texas and they did want to make some money! Because the type of band changed a few times – so did the musicians. As one guitar player left he would be quickly replaced by another eager smiling face so, at times, there was a revolving door of people coming and going in the band.

Also in the late '80's my parents owned a packaged ice company. They operated out of a purpose built ice plant located at the back of the two acres they lived on out in the country. My brother's band room was conveniently located on those two acres too. Due to the nature of the ice business and the convenience of having all those boys fluttering around Mom and Dad often found it useful to have the band members work for them too. Our parents were always happy to let the boys work around their hours if they needed to leave early for a gig or festival then it was always okay. So, it worked out well for everyone. I too worked there off and on so became familiar with some of the guys working at the ice plant. There was one boy in particular that Spirit wanted to make me aware of though. I would find out later that Spirit was using this as a learning experience for me. Back at the end of the 80's there was a popular television program called 'America's Most Wanted'. It had a very distinctive theme tune and when it came on you automatically knew what the program was. We watched this program with great interest on many occasions often wondering if we would see someone we knew and laughed about all the 'rogues' in Mike's band.

Well, it came to be that every time this one band member in particular was around me I would hear the theme tune to America's Most Wanted. It was playing in my head and I could hear it loud and clear! After this happened a few times I did become a little concerned and decided to have a talk with my mom about it. You see the ice company was pretty much a cash business. Every delivery that was made was usually collected for, on delivery, in cash. So, pretty much everyone knew that my mom carried a lot of cash in her handbag until the next day when she would deposit the money at the local bank. The next time I was at my mother's house I told her about what was happening every time I was around this one particular guy and that I was hearing this theme tune from America's Most Wanted. He was a nice enough guy actually and he had buckets full of manners but I wasn't prepared to just let this slide after everything else I had been shown all those years leading up to this point. My mom assured me she would be careful and it was decided that they would even start locking the house when they weren't home. I told you it was the '80's and they lived out in the country. They were notorious for leaving the house unlocked in case anyone wanted to come in for a cold drink or something to eat!

A few days passed and my mother phoned me one afternoon very excited! "Guess what!? You were right again!"

I had forgotten our earlier talk about hearing America's Most Wanted when this boy was around and I asked, "Right about what, Mom?"

She said, "You were right Michelle. Guess what happened? John (not his real name) was on his way to town in his car and a Trooper (Texas State Police) was following him. John had a tail light out and the Trooper pulled him over to tell him about that. You will never guess! He ran his license and he is *wanted* in Houston on a drugs charge! Can you believe that? He's wanted for skipping bail or something."

I was shocked! Yet again Spirit had taken the opportunity to teach me a little something in the way they can communicate with us about things that are going on in our lives. It turned out that John had not showed up for a court date and he had to go back to Houston, courtesy of the State Police, to clear up a few things. But, he did turn out to be a good boy and he's still hanging around now and again even today.

So, pay attention my friends to those hints you may get from Spirit that we don't always take notice of. They may be trying to teach you something. They may be trying to give you an important message about people around you or help protect someone you love who is perhaps far too trusting at times. Try to take notice of things that keep repeating. You will find it is a message from someone in the spirit world trying to communicate with you. You don't have to tell anyone – just pay attention. Write it down – date it. Then see what happens. By writing it down and making an effort to listen you are demonstrating to Spirit that you are accepting their assistance and you are willing to learn. You are willing to communicate with them. When this happens you will find that more and more effort will be made on Spirit's part to communicate with you and build really strong and effective relationship.

"In three words I can sum up everything I've learned about life.

It goes on."

—Robert Frost
(1874 – 1963)
American Poet

9. Heaven – And Back Again!

(Story to cover photo)

July 20, 2005, my Dad went in for a routine surgery which was classed as a 'day case'. This meant he would check himself into the hospital that morning, have his minor operation during the day and then go home in the afternoon when he got the all-clear from the doctors. What a simple plan. My Mother phoned me that morning from Texas, which was 6 hours earlier than me in England, to say they were all checked in to the hospital and that Dad was waiting his turn for the operating room. We chatted for a bit and then Mom put Dad on the phone to say 'Hello' then he put Mom back on. I could hear the nervousness in his voice but I told him I loved him like I always did. It's so funny and I wonder how many other families have the same ritual of having that 'one last talk' on the phone just in case things don't go as planned. Well, this time they weren't wrong. Mom said she would phone me back later that evening to let me know when they got home from the hospital. If I am honest I will say that from the time we hung up that morning I totally forgot about Dad being at the hospital. I had said a little prayer for Dad's safety and after that it's pretty much up to Great Spirit to take over for me and so I went about my day as usual. I finished my day at the office and then it was time to go fetch the children and start the evening chores of feeding, bathing and bedtime. I had a lot on my mind at the time.

Early afternoon I picked up the twins (8 months old) and Xara (3 years old) from nursery and we made our way home through the normal heavy city traffic. My mobile phone rang and I answered it on the hands free speaker; it was Mom. Everything was fine and Dad was in the recovery room. She said as soon as he was up and around they would keep him a couple of hours and then they would be off home. Mom asked how the children were as she always did. Of course, the boys were already asleep in their car seats and Xara chatted away but Mom could never understand her English accent and so it was time to hang up after I had repeated everything Xara had chirped at Mom and Mom would just laugh back at her. I had not driven very far in the heavy afternoon traffic when the phone rang and it was Mom. Once again I took the call on the hands free speaker as I was still driving. I didn't even get to say 'hello' before Mom was shouting down the line,

"Michelle, they can't wake Daddy up. They've taken him into the Intensive Care Unit but they can't wake him up! What do I do? I don't know what to do! He won't wake up!"

I told Mom the first thing she needed to do was calm down. My Dad had been a heart patient for several years and I had hoped that Mom would have sort of gotten used to the idea that *maybe* one day my, normally very lucky, Dad's luck might run out. I didn't want to think about it either and just tried to calm my mom down. I told her, "Just stay calm Mom. Tell me what's happened?"

Mom calmed down a little and stopped shouting but was still very excited as she explained, "They brought him out of surgery and he seemed okay. The doctor came out and said they were just going to wake him up and take him to the recovery room to watch him for awhile and they would let me know when we could leave. But, now they can't get him to wake up and they've put him on a ventilator. OH! Here comes the doctor – I'll call you back."

I couldn't believe Mom had just hung up on me! And because she was in the hospital every time I tried to phone her back it went straight off to a recorded message. I was still driving my small children home and my mind was racing because I needed to know what was happening. I started to pray and anything else I could think to do in my helpless situation. Then, the phone rang again and it was my brother Mike,

"Michelle, it doesn't look good. Dads on a ventilator – the doctor has said to 'call in the family' because Dad is going down really fast. I…I just don't think he's going to make it. They are also trying to locate a heart machine to put him on. It really doesn't look good – I see the Dr. – I will call you back in a bit." Then *HE* hung up! My frustration level was really elevated at this point. I was finding it hard to believe that my Dad was deteriorating so quickly. It had gone from a routine day case surgery to needing to put him on life support. The whole situation seemed so far out of reality that I was having trouble believing it was really happening.

Eventually arriving home I unloaded the children straight from the car into their high chairs in the kitchen for their dinner. I phoned my husband at work and told him what was going on and he said he would be home soon to help me with the kids. I was pacing back and forth in the kitchen trying to think what to do about my family 5000 miles away while getting my children's dinner ready for them. Then, as I was pacing back and forth, I got a very clear vision of my Dad. I could see him very clearly in the spirit world. I could see the white ethereal mist all around him and I could also see my sister Michawn who had passed 17 years earlier in that car wreck I previously told you about! I saw Dad standing with her and talking but I could not hear what they were talking about. I was still pacing around the kitchen taking care of the children while watching this vision in my head so I started talking out loud to Dad, "Dad, you need to come back. Dad, Mom still needs you – we all still need you. Please Dad, be strong and COME BACK." The children were pawing at the finger foods I had given them and watching me walk back and forth while shouting at the ceiling. This seemed to continue for a few minutes and then the phone rang and it was my brother again.

"Michelle, it doesn't look good. They are still looking for a heart lung machine but I don't know if it will get here in time."

I stopped Mike from speaking and told him all that I had just witnessed in my vision and added, "Mike, whatever you do please don't let them turn Dad off. I have a feeling he is going to get to come back so please don't let them turn him off."

Mike stopped me there and said, "OK, I'm going – I won't let them turn him off. Call you later. Love you."

I'm sure if my children could remember that day they would tell people how their excited mother was pacing around the kitchen shouting at the ceiling for some guy to *come back*. It was about that time my husband, Ajaz, arrived home. I was asking him a range of questions from – 'what do you think will happen' to 'should I pack or should I book a ticket home?' What would I do with the kids? I couldn't haul three babies all the way to Texas on my own. I couldn't just leave them while I 'rushed' 5000 miles home for an emergency. A twenty hour trip, one way, isn't exactly rushing! I was really expecting the worse at that point and constructing all these little contingency plans in my head – in case this happens I will do that – what if? How far? How much? Nappies? I was having flashbacks to Michawn dying and all the heartache Dad had gone through when she had died so tragically. He was so mad at that time that he had smashed his fist into the wall and broke his hand. Everything was flooding in on me all at once. I would swell up and cry and then I would pull myself together again as I continued to tend to cleaning up grubby dinner babies and start bath time. All the while silently praying for God to take care of my Dad and bring him back to us.

Finally the phone rang and I was expecting the worst news possible since I had already saw that Dad had passed into the spirit world. It was Mike on the phone and I held my breath as be started to talk. His tone was very somber and reserved as though he couldn't bear to tell me his news.

"Michelle, you will never believe what's happened." And then he paused for effect!

"What? Mike – tell me!" I could hardly breathe the words out.

"You will never believe it Michelle. You know you told me to not let them turn Dad off. Well, I went right to the ICU and put a chair next to him and started talking. I didn't know what else to do. I told him we all needed him and that he needed to come back. I said he couldn't leave us all yet and that Mom still needed him too. I just kept telling him he needed to come back and then you will never believe what happened." And, then he paused for effect again! I could have reached through the phone and strangled Mike myself! Then he finally told me the unbeliev-able truth, "He opened his eyes."

I gasped a breath and then in disbelief I whispered, "You're kidding?"

Mike went on to tell me the most amazing story, "Dad opened his eyes and the nurses started pulling the tubes and stuff off him so he could breathe on his own. He just looked around in disbelief. Mom hurried over to his bedside while the doctors and nurses assembled around the end of his bed. They all wanted to hear what he had to say. Dad looked up at Mom and said – 'I've just been talking to Michawn.' And then he went on to tell *this* story…"

Dad said, "As they wheeled my bed into the ICU – I floated up out of my body - up to the ceiling. I could see my body in the bed and I could see everyone in the room and I could hear them but I couldn't do anything about any of it. Then, I floated up through the ceiling and as I came out the top of the ceiling I was in a beautiful garden. It was the most beautiful garden I have ever seen. Just off in the distance I became aware of a lady walking toward me and when she got closer I could see it was Michawn. I asked her – "Michawn, where am I?" And she said, "Well Dad, you're not quite in Heaven. You're not quite in Heaven because it's not your time to go yet."

Mike took a deep breath as his amazing story continued, "Dad then goes on to tell that he talked with Michawn for what seemed like a very long time although he has no recollection now of what they talked about. She then turned to go back to where ever it is she is residing at this time and, well, Dad turned to go with her because he didn't know what else to do. Michawn turned back around to face Dad, looked him right in the eyes and said, 'Go back, Mother needs you.' That's when he woke up in the ICU."

I was still hanging on Mike's every word on the telephone, "Now, by this time you can imagine Dad had the attention of everyone in that room! Then from the end of the bed one of the Doctors laughed. I gave him a dirty look and asked him, "You think this is funny?" The doctor saw how serious I was and laughed again and said, "Look around you (motioning to look around the ICU), we are surrounded by death. Everyone in here is very close to dying. But, we hear this sort of story all the time. I'm laughing because there is hope even beyond this place we are in. I'm not making fun of your Dad. I believe him because I hear this all the time." They then asked us to leave so they could monitor Dad and get things in the ICU back to a sort of 'normal.'"

Yet again, Spirit had totally amazed me. Not only was I shown a vision of my dad passing over to spirit and given the message that he would be able to return – but Dad came back from that visit and told the exact same story! Does that blow your mind or what? I'm just glad we got the message in time and had the faith to work together to have a happy ending – this time.

Q – How can I know what I see is true? Is it all in my mind?

A - Well, yes it is! Your mind is the link between your physical body and your spirit along with the spirit world. That's not to say you are just imagining what you are receiving/seeing though. You have to develop your relationship with Spirit and learn what it sounds like, feels like, looks like, and smells like when you are having Spirit communication. You must make observations when talking to real life people in order to learn what is going on around you. You have to learn if you can trust certain living people by what they say and do – and the same is true for Spirit. You have to build up a trusting relationship. Then you begin to understand what is real and what the extra chatter in your mind is. You will also begin to understand if there are better times for you to have Spirit communication. Some people seem to relax and connect when they meditate. Others have a very hard time meditating but find that they make quite good connections when they are cooking or driving or doing the ironing. Anything you do that helps you to relax and let go is going to be the best way for you to connect. Just pay attention and you will be surprised at how many times during the course of a day Spirit are trying to communicate with you.

Have you ever had the same thought keep popping into your head? Or do you hear in your head some song and then as soon as you turn on the radio that's the very song that's playing? Have you ever been woken in the night by a nudge or by a voice? Can you smell the perfume of a beloved Grandmother that hasn't been produced for 20 years? Can you see flashes of light out of the corner of your eye or do you notice colorful balls of light on your digital photos? These are all forms of spirit communication. The list is endless. Just pay attention. Every day can be a learning experience if you allow it to be.

Six months after this event, in December, my family came from Texas to visit us once again in England. It was the first time Mike, and his wife Tammy, had ever been here and it was also the first time they were meeting all three of our little children. Mom and Dad came too and one evening we were all in the front room playing around and taking pictures. (You will hear more about pictures in the chapter called Computer Problems!) So there I was snapping pictures so we would always have some dear memories of having the whole family together once again. Since it was Christmas – it was also the anniversary of Russ and Michawn passing into spirit too. I noticed Dad over in the chair nodding off as others watched television and we played with the cameras. I think it was because Dad had come so close to dying I was particularly taking more photos of him than anyone and then – it happened. CLICK. I looked at the display on the digital camera and I couldn't believe the two balls of light I saw – one on each side of my sleeping Dad. I held the camera up. I zoomed in. I held it over to Mom, who was sitting on the sofa next to me, and said, "Hey! Look at that. What do you think that is?" I took it straight in to the computer and downloaded it so we could see a bigger version of it on the monitor. Oh my days! The picture that is on the front cover of this book is the picture I took that day – in my front room at Christmas. The white orb to the left of the photo is Dad's guardian angel and the colorful orb on the right of the photo is filled with spirit family visiting. If you look closely you can see a face (or two) in the colorful orb of light. Our family has differing opinions as to whom it is visiting that Christmas evening but, it doesn't matter to me. I'm just glad they came and I'm even more glad that we were taking pictures at that exact moment!

"The good guest is almost invisible, enjoying him or herself, communing with fellow guests, and, most of all, enjoying the generous hospitality of the hosts."

—Emily Post (1872 – 1960)
American authority of social behaviour

10. The Guest Room

We have an extra room in our house that we've always referred to, affectionately, as the guest room. Not just because this is the designated room where living people sleep when they come to visit – say – from the USA but it's also a room that seems to have quite a lot of spirit guests too. Before the children came along we referred to that area of the house as 'The East Wing'. Well, it is facing east even if it isn't a full wing. It's just not in alignment with the rest of the house which makes it sort of feel like it's out on its own wing I guess.

Ajaz and I spent quite a lot of time driving around on weekends to find a house to buy. Eighteen months to be exact! But, when we found it we just knew it was what we were looking for. Within hours of locating this property we had arranged for a viewing and shook hands on the full asking price. Now, anyone who knows my husband will tell you that the full asking price is just a complete no-no to him. But, for whatever the reason was he just had to have *this* house. We were able to move in quite quickly even though we had absolutely no furnishings. We didn't mind as we've always been a bit picky and enjoyed shopping for furniture and things on our weekends off work. For the whole first year we lived in this four bedroom home we had pretty much no furnishings. We seemed to work all the time so a bed and television in our room seemed to do us just fine. I used the guest room as my dressing room. It has a massive walk-in closet so who in their right mind wouldn't want to use all that space? That was my private boudoir and it also had a dressing table, with hair and makeup supplies, which was perfect for getting ready for work each day.I suppose the tension from working together and never having a great deal of leisure time finally got to us when we had lived here about 10 months. I don't remember what the big argument was about – maybe a bit of it was me missing my family and Texas – but who can say at this point. One harsh word led to another and amidst the bitter exchange of words I finally said, "I'm going back to Texas." I waited for Ajaz to plead with me to stay but the only words he could manage were, "Good, I'm glad. Go back."

Well, that was all I needed to hear. Up the stairs I went to pack all my worldly belongings. It didn't actually amount to much so the job wouldn't take long at all. I had my mind set. I was definitely leaving. I would pack up and maybe even try to make the flight the next morning. Nothing was stopping me. Nothing.

I got to the closed guest room door and went to turn the handle to go in. I heard a terrible grinding noise unlike anything I've ever heard before. The door handle came off inside the door. Then the handle in my hand swung free as though not connected to anything at all. The door would not open. Never had I ever seen anything like it before.

I turned to go back downstairs and was met by Ajaz coming up. "Aren't you getting your stuff?" he asked bluntly.

I told him, "I would but the door won't open." So, I went downstairs. I didn't know what to do at that point. I picked up the phone and called my brother in law to tell him what an unreasonable so-and-so his brother was being. "Oh dear, I will be right over." He said.

Ajaz came downstairs and picked up the telephone next. I asked him what he was doing and he said he was phoning a locksmith! I asked him, "A locksmith, and what for?"

He said, "To fix the door so you can leave!" My heart sank a little.

My oldest brother in law, Shahzad, arrived well before the locksmith who took about an hour to get here. Shahzad calmed down the situation as the locksmith worked on the door upstairs. Finally, the door was fixed but the locksmith had one very interesting thing to add as he handed Ajaz the bill for putting on a new lock, "I've never seen anything like that in all my days."

Ajaz looked at him funny as he furrowed his thick eyebrows and said, "What's that?"

"That lock was exploded from the *inside* of the lock. I've never seen that before – ever." He then looked at me as I think he had heard a bit of what had been being discussed as he worked and he said, "I don't think someone wanted you to leave." And he smiled as he walked out the door. His words went through my head a few times as I looked over at Ajaz. Ajaz looked back at me and that was all I needed to hear as I decided I would stay. Spirit wanted me in England for some reason.

Slowly, over time, the guest room had finally been decked out with a bed and furnishings. There would be the odd need sometimes - here and there - for me to sleep in that room. If Ajaz had a cold he would snore exceptionally loud so there would be times I would sleep in the guest room out of a pure selfish need for sleep.My parents would come to visit us every six months or so and each time they came Mom would bring along some little trinket I had left behind in the States. They've always been good about hauling my junk around for me but on this one particular occasion they brought me a little treasure Michawn had given me a couple of years before she passed away. It was one of those funny little porcelain figures with two cow characters dressed up like a cowboy and a cowgirl. They were having a high old time at the dancehall or something and holding beer bottles above their heads and laughing (the cows – not Mom and Dad). The little wind up music box had a sliding side – to – side mechanism on the back you could push over to one side when you wanted to start or stop the tune that played "How Dry I Am". My children loved to wind it up and let it play itself all the way out until it slowly dragged out the last tinkle…..tinkle…tin…k…le…tink.

So, one night after trying to sleep with the snoring machine in full force next to me I decided I would need to go to the guest room if I was going to get any sleep that night. I often read for a little bit before turning off the light and going to sleep. Anyone who has ever slept in the guest room will tell you it's the best night's sleep you will ever have. It's just so calm and peaceful in that room. So, I fell asleep right away as was usual. It seemed like several hours had gone by when I was woke up – to the sound of the music box on the side table. It was tinkling out – in full force I might add – "How Dry I Am, How Dry I Am, Nobody Knows – How Dry I Am." It was as if someone had wound the mechanism up fully and then pushed the switch to the side to start the music box playing that familiar tune. I did not get up. I was not afraid although I did turn over and look to see if anyone was there – it's just a normal reaction I think. Of course no one was there so I laid my head back down and listened as the music box finally ran itself out…. tinkle…..tinkle……tink.

Michawn has made herself known a few other times in that room too. She seems to like that room for some reason! One time in particular I had her on my mind – I often hear the theme tune to the movie "Beaches" when she is near. Well, that tune was playing in my head as I walked into the guest room to get dressed one morning. I said out loud, "Hello Michawn." Immediately the overhead light in the room flickered a strange sort of flicker. This had never happened before in all the many years we had lived there so I said, "If that's you Michawn please make the light flicker again." Immediately the light flickered that strange flickery flicker like you see on television. I thanked her and continued getting dressed. Soon the 'Beaches' tune faded from my head. She must have had other things to be getting on with too and just stopped by to say good morning.

The last thing I will share with you about the guest room is a time when Mom was visiting. Of course she was staying in the guest room. I had told her previously some of the things that had happened in there and she was really hoping to see/hear/feel close to Michawn too. I can tell you from previous experience of giving readings to people that it's typical when someone desperately wants a reading or communication with a particular spirit that they unintentionally block that communication. Strange, I know, but that's how it seems to work for me at least. If you will relax – send out your love to the person you want to hear from – you have a better chance of getting a reading at a demonstration too. Well, Mom was unpacking and had taken some hangers out of the wardrobe and put them on the bed. As she was standing there she said it looked to her like an invisible 'someone' had flopped right down on the bed and the hangers went flying all over the bed! She stood for a split second in amazement then she said, "Michawn is that you?!" She stood for a moment more and heard no reply and then began to cry as she held her face in her hands. Just then she says it felt as though someone had taken their arms and wrapped them around her. She felt comforted and felt as though Michawn was giving her a great big hug. Mom felt better and composed herself. Even now, when she tells this story she gets covered with goose bumps. It's a story that gives her a lot of comfort I know because it's true we cannot make ourselves get the goose bumps. When you tell a story and get goose bumps – it's a confirmation of the truth. It's an inbuilt truth detector. Try it!

"Always do the best you can and God will give you credit for the rest. He's a smart guy."

—Michelle Rathore – Spirit Nudges: Proof that Spirit is
Never Far Away
American Artist/Author
(1965 -)

11. Random Spirit Visitors

One of the main themes running through my search for the truth was wondering why some spirits came to visit me – some of them had absolutely no message. They were just there and I could see them. Sometimes they came to me with a tiny message for someone I knew and there has been one friend of mine that spirit seem to know will always get their messages passed along to her. 'Shell' came to work for our family business when I was expecting Xara back in 2002. I was hoping to go off on maternity leave and not return to work but, I am glad that I did if only to get to know her better.

Having had many conversations with Shell and getting to know each other we developed a trusting relationship. Many years ago she and I were the only two ladies in the office so we passed occasional breaks in the day's monotony just chatting about different aspects of our lives. Shell came to know a bit more about me and seemed to understand and be very accepting of my spiritual viewpoint. I would suppose that being witness to many strange goings on in our very old office building went a good way to supporting her belief in my spiritual views too. Back then we had a 'ghost' called 'Pastor Rowe' who would randomly turn things off; the vacuum cleaner and a commercial sewing machine to name a few occurrences that come to mind. I would have to say that Shell pays attention to her psychic side as she has told me a number of things that have happened to her as well. So, when I've relayed certain information or messages to Shell over the years she has always been accepting even it was to take a 'wait and see' attitude.

Shell's wedding day came and went with the all the joy and flair she is so well known for. Then we waited for the day Shell would come and announce the pitter patter of little feet which finally trumpeted through her usual broad smile and jolly laugh quickly followed by a succession of clapping hands and a little cheer. She had a mixture of feelings as I am sure most newly expectant mothers do. Several months had passed and one evening while I was at home I got a connection to Shell's unborn baby. I thought it was brilliant! So, I started texting Shell, "Hey, baby is telling me that you've been eating something that's churning around in your tummy."

Shell text back, "LOL! That's right!"

I had one more brief message from baby which I reluctantly relayed via text to Shell again, "Baby says you need to open a window."

The reply was one of great laughter! Indeed baby was correct. Oh, how indignant to tell off on your expectant mummy like that!Then as the years rolled by Shell found her relationship with her husband on a rocky path. This sometimes happens to parents who find the stresses of work and family life a bit hard going especially after there is a new baby combined with poor health factored in too. Sadly my lovely friend was now going through a divorce. Understandably she was having a really terrible time juggling work and a baby as well as planning out her life and all that it might hold for her without her long time husband at her side. Month after month went by and Shell would keep me posted on the progress of the divorce. I could tell it was the hardest thing she had probably ever had to endure and then one week she told me, "Well, my divorce is final next week. I guess I will be free and single. I hope it's what he really wants because it's what he's going to get now."

I was really sad for Shell and she did pull at my own heart-strings. I couldn't imagine what it would be like to have to start life over again, on my own, especially with a small baby in tow. I went home and the weekend took my mind off to other matters as I had my own three small children to run around after.

I have to say I am always a bit relieved when Sunday night rolls around. The prospect of the children all going back to school on Monday is a blessed event! As I stepped into the shower that Sunday evening relaxing and enjoying the hot steamy water my mind decided to take me on a very quick journey. My mind connected right up with my lovely friend, Shell. I could see her very clearly and right above her head was a beautiful, perfect, gold wedding ring spinning gently suspended in air. It was so over-sized and completely perfect! It was about the size of a car tire above her head but there was no mistaking that it was a perfect gold wedding band. Then, as quickly as it had appeared, it was gone. I filed the image away to tell Shell the next day.

That Monday morning I dropped the kids off at school and made my way to the office. I have to say that with the commotion that a Monday morning brings in the office I had let the whole vision completely slip my mind. It was probably mid-morning when I remembered what I had been shown the night before in the shower.

Through the open office doorway I asked, "Shell? Tell me again what's going on with your divorce."

Shell looked at me a bit puzzled. She knew this was my tone of '*I'm leading up to something*.'

Shell said, "I've spoken with my solicitor and I am going over on Thursday to sign the divorce papers. It will all be done and dusted by Friday." She cocked her head sideways and smirked at me. "What do you know? *Why* do you ask?"

I was a little confused because of the vision I had been shown the night before but I knew I was going to tell her anyway so I didn't drag it out. "I was taking a shower last night and you came to mind." Shell roared with laughter as she threw her head back, "Oh *do* tell!" Shell does make me laugh!

"Well, I was taking a shower and I could see a big golden wedding band spinning right above your head. I thought maybe something had happened that you forgot to tell me about?"

Shell was really looking at me cockeyed by this point. "What does *that* mean?"

I was very honest and told Shell I didn't know what it meant but it was a beautiful perfect wedding band spinning above her head. I was so sure it was something positive and that's why I wanted to know if anything had happened that she had forgot to tell me about. So, we left it at that like so many other things we've discussed in passing just waiting to see what might come of it.

A couple of days passed and Thursday came around. I went into the office as usual but I knew something was different. I put my coat away and went in to sit down at my desk. Seeing Shell through the open doorway sitting at her desk I was very surprised to see a smile beaming from ear to ear.

"OH MY GOD, Michelle you will never guess what happened last night!" She was so animated and smiling so widely I was just happy to see her filled with joy after having been so depressed for so many months while processing her divorce. "What? Tell me!" I could hardly wait to hear her news.

"Well, my *nearly* Ex came over to watch Livvy (their baby Olivia) last night because I was going to the cinema with Cheryl (her sister). He showed up at the door on his knees – crying – saying *I WANT MY WIFE AND BABY BACK!*"

By this point Shell was hysterical with laughter. She told me how he had made a big show of wanting her back and telling her that he just couldn't go through with the divorce. He said his life was a total misery without his two girls and begged for them to work things out. He said he had made this big decision over the weekend and found it hard to wait until Wednesday night to tell her. It had taken him that long to work up the courage!

Somehow Spirit already knew and they had let me and Shell in on the secret during my shower on Sunday night. I am happy to report my lovely friend is still happily married and I sure hope she never has to go through anything like that again in her life.

But, of course, we cannot forget all the visits I have had from Shell's beloved grandmother. Most recently she popped in with the intention of connecting with Shell about her daughter, Olivia. Once again I texted Shell, "Has Olivia started having temper tantrums yet?"

Shell quickly replied, "OH MY GOD! Yes she has!! LOL!"

This is something I would not have known about as I had been off work for several weeks and working from home. I told Shell, "Your Grandma says she is *just like you!*"

I could just see Shell at her desk laughing as she replied, "Absolutely!" We had a longer conversation face to face later on in which Shell was telling me she had spoken to her parents over the weekend and her dad was making fun of how much Olivia was like Shell when she was growing up. Evidently Shell used to throw some amazing tantrum displays and Shells dad was happy to tell her, "What goes around comes around." I'm quite sure there are other tidbits I have left out that I've told Shell about over the years but these are just a few of the times that Spirit was happy to pop in and say hello knowing that their little messages would be passed on and that Shell and her family would happily accept those messages as they were intended; with love.

So I've had loads of little visitors all going back to when I was small. Some would just stand and stare at me and then disappear. Some I can see as they seem to walk down the hall – appearing through a wall and then evaporating into thin air. When

I was about twenty I remember waking up and there was a man standing next to the bed who was dressed in the same sort of outfit like Benjamin Franklin would have worn. It wasn't Ben Franklin but gosh he sure looked like him. He was standing on the right side of the bed and as I raised my head off the pillow I looked down toward my feet, at the end of the bed, I could see a small boy of about nine or ten years old standing there too. He had black hair and was wearing one of those white cotton night shirts from about the same era as this man standing next to me. I looked at both of them; one and then the other. I was wide awake and I waited for them to either say something or do something – anything. But, they just stood there looking at me so I figured it was a bit useless just all of us watching each other and I turned over and went back to sleep. To this day I don't know what they wanted. Perhaps they were just part of my journey and helping me to understand that we can see spirit without being afraid. Maybe they were keeping an eye on me for some other reason? I honestly don't know but I will never forget seeing them that night.

"God doesn't require us to succeed; he only requires that you try."

—Mother Teresa of Calcutta (1910 - 1997)
Winner of the Nobel Peace Prize 1979

12. Baby Name Readings

Having had success doing readings in the Spiritualist Church I soon found myself getting requests from people outside of the church as well. These came from various places; friends, family, a-friend-of-a-friend was quite common too. But, soon I was receiving emails from people I didn't know and I wasn't too sure where they got my name from either. Maybe it was from Facebook or any of the other social media sites we all rush to be a part of now days. When I first started doing readings for others I found it hard to charge very much for my services. This is a problem quite a few spiritual people have when they are offering their services to others. We find it hard to place a value on our work because, often times, we don't have anyone else to compare ourselves to. If you go buy a loaf of bread in the store you kind of know what to anticipate for that sliced up hunk of carbs. There are several other loaves on offer and you choose which variation you want then go check out and pay. You chose exactly what you wanted and went to the till and paid for it. Your anticipation isn't very high because you've bought bread before. You already know pretty much how it will taste and what you can do with it. Sandwich? Toast? Breadcrumbs for a casserole? You see what I mean. But, when someone wants a reading from a psychic or a medium you aren't very sure exactly what is going to come of it. Will the sitter want to know about their future, a faithful spouse, a job prospect, their own undeveloped gifts or perhaps they want to know if they will ever have children, etc. Sometimes when you have a mediumship reading the person you are hoping to hear from in spirit doesn't show up as requested. Just because *you* are ready to talk doesn't mean *they* are. So there are a lot of variables to try to factor in. I like to just leave the reading as open as possible and see what either spirit or your Angels and guides may think is the most important message for you to receive. Most people are very happy to start this way too. I guess it takes the pressure off them asking a particular question. The readings normally turn out just fine starting on this platform.

As I wanted everyone to be happy with the readings I was doing when I first started out I decided to charge very little. I felt this took some performance pressure off me I guess but I was soon to find out that this had backfired on me. I found the more readings I did and the more success I had that my inbox was really becoming a bit hard to manage. I was being recommended to others and I certainly had not planned on that for some strange reason. The really strangest thing of all was that I seemed to be focusing on unborn babies at that time. I think it all started when a lady who was expecting a baby emailed me for a reading. She was wanting to know if everything was going to be okay but also asked to leave the reading open so if any of her family in spirit wanted to come through with a message she could receive that as well.

I started her reading and quickly made a connection with an energy which I felt to be her unborn baby. As I know we are all spirit whether it is before we are born, when we are here or after we pass back into the spirit world I had requested to be connected to the energy of this lady's unborn child. I had her permission to do this of course. I had the impression of a boy's name the baby would like to be called as well as other things the baby could hear going on in the house around his mother. I told her the baby could hear a strange sounding name being called quite a lot. Well it sounded strange to me so I sounded it out for her – Am uh lee. I thought it sounded a bit like *Emily* but the baby kept correcting me every time I said the name wrong. The baby was showing me pink, pink, pink and the feeling of a ballerina dancing. Then I had the happiest smiling frog face I've ever seen just pop right up at me. I was really thrown back a bit wondering why I would be seeing a smiling frog. It's normally in our nature to just let these little tidbits in life go out of our head and ignore them as though it's bits of nonsense floating through our day but, I know from past experience that I am supposed to give my client exactly what spirit is showing me. I am not to add to any of the information and I am not to take away from any of the information. Sometimes what I pass on has no meaning at that specific moment to the client but often I will get an email back, sometimes days or weeks later, saying they either remember what that particular bit was about or it has come to pass.

So I emailed this nice lady back explaining I had connected with her unborn child and describing all this little one wanted to express. I told her that the baby was aware of celebrations and giving me the color pink over and over again as though it covered everything. I also told her that I was getting a name that sounded like *Emily* but that the baby kept correcting me that I was saying the name wrong. So I wrote it out phonetically as *Am-uh-lee* but I wasn't sure if that was right as I had never heard that name before. I wondered, as we sometimes do, if I was making this name up. And, knowing I had to include everything I had received I also told her about the smiling frog face. Even though it was spirit who showed me all the information I was still a little hesitant about including it but boy was I glad I did!Not long after hitting the 'send' button I received an excited email in return. She could not believe I had gotten *that* name! As she was heading out the door to work I was promised another email in the next few hours so, with a pleased smile, I went about my day waiting to hear more news from this expectant mom.

After a few hours I did indeed receive another email telling me how I had gotten so much of the reading spot on and asking even more questions. She wanted to let me know that the baby's cousin – a very girly girl – had just had a pink, pink, pink birthday party. Evidently everything had to be pink for this little girl and they had made the party into a dress-up or costume party. Princess Pinky wore her ballerina outfit which was, of course, **pink** while her cousin (this unborn baby's older brother) wore a frog costume! Perhaps as though thinking I may not believe her I was also emailed a photo of the smiling frog. The hat to this costume was a full frog's head which you inserted your own head inside. Just inside the wide open frogs mouth was a very wide mouthed grin of a sweet little boy smiling back. There, indeed, was my smiling frog. And, just one more bit of info to come and complete the puzzle. What was the name the baby was telling me about? Well, it would appear that Princess Pinky's name was Amalea and her cousin, the smiling frog, kept shouting her name all day. Amalea! Amalea!

Yet again spirit never ceases to amaze me with the information that will come through from a reading. We already know from scientists that babies can hear what is going on around them in the form of pots banging and dogs barking as well as responding to people's voices and soothing music but, I was astonished that I was given colors and a smiling frog as though the baby was also aware visually of what was going on around them too.

I've had so many amazing baby readings that I could never have enough room here to share them all. One baby told off on his anonymous mother. I could see footballs (English soccer balls) all around this baby and a certain team's colors too. I told this 'mum' that I was given a very strong connection to football and that this child would definitely be a professional footballer one day. I immediately got a reply that although she was unable to tell me who she was that, indeed, her husband was a professional player and her father-in-law had been a pro too. She added that there was absolutely no way this child would not be a professional football player one day. Of all the people I have read for it would sure be nice to know who that anonymous lady was just to watch that little striker in the future and think, "I remember him from before he was born."

"Faith is believing in something when common sense tells you not to."

—From the movie 'Miracle of 34th Street'
Written & Directed by George Seaton

13. Computer Problem

Having three children under the age of three makes it a certainty that the camera is out and there are lots of pictures being taken. I had gotten a digital camera so we could download all the photos and not have to print each and every infinitesimally slightly different picture we took. It just made sense to me to take all the photos we wanted and put them straight on the computer for safe keeping especially after all the heartache it took to get our three little ones here. Our precious only girl, Xara, who took three rounds of IVF before we got pregnant and then another round of IVF found us ready to have twins! Gosh! You can imagine the amount of photos on that computer. We also took photos of other family members and always uploaded everything just in case the camera got lost or broken we wouldn't lose any of them.

Everywhere we went we took that camera. On the day Xara was born my father-in-law, Altaf, unexpectedly died. In fact, he died and four hours later Xara was born in a hospital across town. It was a bittersweet day indeed. So, realizing how quickly someone could leave this earth, we took even more photos! And, we kept uploading all of them to the hard drive of our computer. (You can see where this is leading can't you?)

We diligently took photos at the weekend when family was

around. We clicked away when our oldest niece was married in London. We really clicked away when the twins came along because they were just so sweet and we were having a time with Xara deciding if she liked them or not. She was two and a half years old when Rocco and Marcus were born and on the day the boys came home from the hospital she made quite a declaration. The boys were side by side on the sofa when Xara came home from nursery that day with Daddy. She marched in with her bottom lip out as Mummy was in the front room paying far too much attention to the newcomers. Xara stomped into the room still in her school uniform, coat and beret cocked to one side of her tiny head. She walked right up to the sofa – stuck her forefinger out shaking it first at one and then the other, "I like *this* one but I don't like *that* one!" We actually got a video of that and shortly after uploaded it to the computer too!

When the twins were six months old my mother-in-law, Balquees, passed away. We quickly realized that she had made herself quite absent in most of the photos we had and so we were glad when we did manage to find a handful of photos from various occasions safely tucked away on the computer.

A few months after Balquees died I went into our home office to work on the computer and found it was switched off. That was unusual as we never turned it off – ever. I would push the 'on' button and some of the lights would flash and then it made a flicky thing on the screen and nothing would happen. Oh the panic! You know how you can just tell when an electrical appliance has got real problems? Well, I could tell. I just couldn't understand – we had not had a power outage and the computer was plugged into a surge protector. There really was no reason to be having a problem with it.

My mind immediately began to race. I was really panicking! I had written half a book that had not been backed up anywhere else and, of course, all our photos where on there too. The only photos of Balquees we had were on that computer!

I then picked up the phone and called Ajaz at work. I told him how the computer wouldn't work and I was really worried as all the photos of his mother were on it. He said to just unhook everything and he would take it in to be looked at the next morning on his way to work. So, that's what I did – and he delivered the computer bright and early the next morning to the little shop around the corner from the office. He asked their Tech Guy to ring us when he found out what was wrong and Ajaz went back to work.

By the time I dropped all the children off at nursery and made my way into the office the bad news had already been phoned in. The Tech Guy had phoned to say the hard disc was fried, the mother board was gone and even the power cord leading into the tower had melted! Part of his diagnosis process was to hook the computer up to a retrieval unit to see if he could save anything off the computer's hard drive. He said that too had failed. My heart sank! How could this possibly happen? So, I picked up the phone and rang the computer guy myself.

I started out talking like a reasonably sane person to this computer techy guy. We went over his diagnosis again and he was kind enough to repeat everything he had already told Ajaz earlier. And then I made my plea, "Please – the only photos of my mother-in-law are on that computer. Every photo we have is there. We have no copies and no backups. Please – can you just try one more time to retrieve our data?" He seemed to detect my desperation over the phone and said he would hook the retrieval unit up before he left for the night and let it run all night. But, he just wanted me to know in advance that he didn't think he was going to get anything because the computer was just in too bad of shape. I thanked him and hung up with a very heavy heart.

I had recently been reading one of Doreen Virtue's books – I think it is called "The Lightworkers Way" – in this book she described how her mother told her one night that "Nothing is lost in the mind of God." Her mother had described how she could find anything that she perceived to be lost because God knew where everything was and all we had to do was ask – and believe in our heart – and it would turn up. So that's what I did.

I began to pray with an earnest heart, "Nothing is lost in the mind of God. Please give me the photos back. Please Angels – nothing is lost in the mind of god. Nothing is lost in the mind of God." I prayed at work. I prayed leaving work. Over and over the same thing and asking to please be allowed to have those pictures back. I prayed on my way to pick up the children and while making dinner and especially when I was going to bed. It was the last thing on my mind while going to sleep and the first thing on my mind the next morning when I woke up.

I began again like a broken record, "Nothing is lost in the mind of God. Please give us the pictures back." Over and over. I dropped off the children at nursery and carried on to work still chanting the same mantra in my head.

When I got to work I asked Ajaz what the computer guy had said. Had he spoken to him yet? Ajaz had been too busy that morning so he asked me to give the man a call and see what was going on. So, I did.

I picked up the phone – still chanting in my head – dialing the numbers....dreading the phone being answered on the other end and excited for someone to answer it!

I said, "Hi – its Michelle here – I was wondering if you were able to salvage anything out of our computer last night?"

And that lovely angel on the other end of the telephone said, "You know – it's the strangest thing I've ever seen. Your computer is fried. I mean really – and the mother board is gone too. So, I did what I told you I would do and I hooked it up last night to the recovery unit. I almost didn't because I knew it wouldn't be able to retrieve anything off the computer because it – it's just gone. But, when I came in this morning and looked at the recovery unit it had retrieved ONE FILE. Guess what? It's a picture file.

I don't know what's on it but I'm backing it up right now and I will get it over to you."

ONE FILE!! ONE!! That was all I had asked for!! That was what I had prayed with an earnest heart for - just that one file with pictures in it. I was thanking every Spirit that could hear me for eternity! My heart was so full and I was sitting there crying because it *is* true!

Nothing is lost in the mind of God. And, come to find out, it was ALL the pictures off the computer. The only photos of my mother in law were there. All the picture of the twins – Xara – everything.

After making sure I had a couple of backup copies of the photos it occurred to me – why didn't I ask for the manuscript too? Well, if I had then I wouldn't have had the chance to include some of the special stories I am sharing with you now. So, in that event, God gave me a really good story to share with you! That's why I didn't get the manuscript back too.

Never forget, nothing is lost in the mind of God – and that includes you.

"The invariable mark of wisdom is to see the miraculous in the common."

—Ralph Waldo Emerson
(1803 – 1882)

14. Harold, Danny and the Coat with No Feet

Before I carry on and tell you about Harold and Danny I think it is important that you know one thing about me and how we operate in our home. Although I have been able to see/hear/ sense/feel spirit all my life – it's natural to me just like breathing. Well, I don't go around talking about it or insisting that everyone believes what I believe. While my children have been small I thought it was important for them to just be allowed to be children. I didn't preach to them about God or spirit. Although, if they asked any questions – like children do – about something like angels then they got as good an answer as I could give them from my understanding on the subject. Granted, my understanding may be just that little bit different than other parents may be. Not better or worse – just different. We have always tried to instill in the children to be good and really the only hard and fast rule I have ever had is – tell the truth. This is a very important standard that I have drilled into them for as long as I can remember. Tell the truth in all things and everything will be okay. I mean, I have a few other rules but I won't bore you with those.

Although I already knew *my* children would be superior in every way to anyone else's children (I'm joking ......uh, not really

– ok, I'm joking) I always knew we would allow them to develop any special gifts they had and then we could support them, if needed, when the time came.

So, when Xara was about seven years old I wasn't surprised to hear her say she could see someone in her room at bedtime. I was, however, surprised to hear her say it was a black man. (This one was Harold) Every night she would ask me why it had to be a man. "Why can't I have a lady angel?" she would say. I would tell her that we didn't really get to choose who we have as angels or guides and that we would have different guides (that's who I thought it was- a guide) at different times in our lives to help us learn certain lessons. She seemed to accept this but it didn't make going to sleep any easier for her. I guess what surprised me when she said it was a black man is that in all my years of dealing with spirit I had never put a color on them. They were just spirit or they were someone's loved one who came with a message – and that was it. Having a color was something that the living had – not spirits. This went on for some time and one Saturday morning I was in the kitchen cooking breakfast when Xara came into the kitchen too. She slowly walked over and tucked herself up under my arm and whispered to me as she looked over toward the breakfast bar, "He's sitting in my chair." She was, of course, referring to a spirit – there were two by this point who regularly made their presence known to her.

I said to Xara, "Well, you should speak to him like any other friend you are trying to get to know. Say hello and ask him what his name is."

She turned to the apparently empty chair and said, "Excuse me please, what is your name?" and then she listened for a moment and turned back to me to repeat what she had just heard, "He says his name is Danny."

I then told Xara, "Well, that's a nice name. Ask him why he is here? Just speak to him like you would any friend you are getting to know."

She turned to the chair again and said, "Excuse me please, why are you here?" She listened again and turned to relay the message to me once more carefully sounding out one word in particular. "He says he is here to *com-fort* and protect me."

I looked at her and smiled. I said, "Well, that sounds okay doesn't it Xara? That really sounds pretty good to me." I turned toward the stove and continued to make breakfast wondering what would happen next. Xara seemed relieved and in a moment she smiled and asked me something I had not been expecting. Sounding out the words carefully she said, "Mummy, what does commm-fort mean?"

That's when it hit me. She was repeating what she was hearing and she didn't even know what it meant. That was all the proof I needed that she was indeed having her own little conversation with one of her spirit guides.

So, time moved on and it was a nightly thing that Xara was telling me about Harold and how he was in her room each night standing next to her bed. She kept asking me why he was there and why couldn't she have a lady yet? I just kept reassuring her that he was there for a good reason and when his work was finished he would go help someone else and she would have a different guide come to help her with something else she might need to learn. I was concerned that *she* was so concerned but I knew she was protected and, besides myself, I had asked a couple of my friends to check 'Harold' out for me too. I was just making sure I wasn't standing too close to the trees to see the forest if you know what I mean. The reports all came back a-ok from everyone so I was content to leave it at that.

Christmas was getting closer and Xara was in the nativity play at school. She had a speaking part and was taking great care to learn all her lines and the special songs that went along with the play. The evening before the play I went upstairs to help her get ready for bed. She went to our bathroom to brush her teeth and I went to the other end of the hall, into her room, to close the curtains and get her bed ready. As I stood there I became aware of Harold standing next to her bed just as she had described. In my mind's eye he appeared to me to look just like one of the Magi out of the Christmas stories. I told him, "I know you are here to help Xara and if I can help – that's why I am here too." As I said that I could feel him move closer and as his aura brushed up against my aura my skin raised up in goose bumps but only on my right side! My *whole* right side that was directly facing him and only my right side – none of the left side! I could hear Xara come skipping down the hall and she was singing one of the Christmas songs she needed to remember for the next day. As she came skipping into her room she looked straight up and in the direction of Harold and exclaimed pointing, "There he is! He's right next to you Mummy!" I smiled and told her I knew he was there and that I had just been speaking with him. Xara seemed okay with that and went to bed with sugar plum fairies dancing in her head.

Life went on and Xara again began to complain that she wanted a lady 'angel'. It still used to get to me that although I was able to communicate with spirit I was really having a tough time communicating with Harold. It's just one of those things. I wondered if I was just tired or stressed from work or was it something else. I did wonder if I was I being prevented from communicating with him for some other reason. You know, mothers can be over protective for a lot of different reasons! This was my daughter and I wanted to know what was going on. I think that's reasonable.

One afternoon I was in the kitchen making dinner – standing at the sink washing something and Harold appeared in front of me. Perhaps he sensed my apprehension too? I thought to myself that I wanted to make very sure that this being who was a frequent visitor in our home was at least of God's Light even if I couldn't find out any more than that and so I made this command right to his face knowing that if he was of God's Light it wouldn't do anything to him. I said, "I command you to go to

God's Highest Light. I command you to go to God's Highest Light. I command you to go to God's Highest Light." Almost before I could get out the last sentence he replied to me, "I Am of God's Highest Light." So, I thought – good enough for me mate – you're welcome then and I felt okay about Harold from then on. It's not for us to have to know everything that's going on I guess. I am just really happy to know that my children are growing up in a house where their spiritual gifts are allowed to flourish and we can help them if they need us to. No subject is off limits and I am sure in the coming months and years that I will learn far more from them than they have ever learned from me. Sometimes it's hard to accept someone or something when it's staring you right in the face as being special or extraordinary. Sometimes we try to just make everything mundane instead of the miracle it actually is. It is okay for us to accept some things we don't understand as being for our higher good – sometimes.

Another one of those Saturday mornings rolled around and found me in the kitchen making French toast again. It's just our little weekend treat so as the children ran around out in the chilly morning air I was happily cooking away at the stove. As Xara came in and slung her coat on the chair I said, "Go put that away in the closet Xara and wash your hands; come help Mummy."

"Well are the boys going to help too? They are still running around outside and they won't listen to me Mummy!" She plopped her hat on top of her coat as she made a dash for the door to look out. As she was looking out the glass doors she complained again, "I told them to pick up that coat in the woodlands but they won't listen."

I chastised her a little as she is the oldest, "Oh, who's took their coat off? It's cold outside Xara you should have made them come in or you should have picked it up and brought it in. We're a family and we look out for each other."

Xara just looked at me with a scowl, "I don't *know* whose coat it is." I was a bit annoyed at that point and replied, "It doesn't matter whose coat it is Xara you should have brought it in. Coats cost money and we have to take care of our things. What color is it?" Even though the boys are twins I always buy them different colored clothes so they can keep track of who owns what. Having collected the knives and forks from the cutlery drawer, Xara began to set the table for breakfast and said, "It's a blue coat Mummy but it's not the boy's coat. I don't know whose coat it is."

I have to say I was actually only half listening as we had this sort of back and forth banter about a blue coat out in the woodland walk. I was trying not to burn the French toast as Xara set the table and got the maple syrup out of the cupboard to inspect the sticky lid with her tongue. She giggled as she cut her eyes to see if I was watching her. I called everyone in for breakfast and we had a hurried shuffle of knives and forks as we all devoured the hot sticky bread. What had taken forty minutes to cook had only taken five minutes to eat! As I started collecting the plates to wash Xara insisted on talking about the coat again, "Isn't anyone going to go see about that coat?"

Once again I wondered out loud as to why she had left the coat in the woods, "You know Xara if the boys saw your coat laying outside I would be upset with them if they didn't bring it in for you. Wouldn't I?"

Xara was starting to really get put out with me, "But, Mummy, it's not the *boys* coat. I don't know *whose* coat it is. It's just *there* in the woods. It's too big for the boys and it doesn't have *any feet.*"

Well now, this did surprise me. I wondered who had been on the woodland walk right next to our home – inside our property – and why on earth they had left their coat there. All sorts of things ran through my head. Was there a stranger walking around in our garden? Did we have a homeless person sleeping next to our home? I put the spatula down and took off my apron as I headed toward the back conservatory door that was leading out to the woodlands, "Come on Xara show me where that coat is."

As we hurriedly walked out the back doors and down the steps to the woodlands I asked Xara, "What do you mean *it doesn't have any feet?*"

As we got to the last step going into the woodlands she quietly said, "There Mummy." And she pointed at a big apple tree at the top of the walk. "The coat was there next to the tree; leaning against it."

I asked Xara if she could still see the coat and she said that she couldn't. Xara just looked at the tree and all around. "It was right here Mummy. It was a blue coat and it was like someone was standing next to the tree and it went all the way to the ground, but not all the way touching the ground, and then it was just hanging there with no feet sticking out the bottom and there was no head coming out the top. It was right here!"

Xara was so insistent all morning that someone needed to go see about the coat outside and then again while standing next to the tree that there is just no way that she didn't see this coat. So, not knowing what else to do I asked her to draw me a picture. Sure enough she drew a picture of a blue tunic style coat with long sleeves hovering near the apple tree. One arm was leaning up against the tree as though someone was relaxing while watching the children play. She drew only a blue coat next to the tree – it was a coat with no feet.

We may not always listen when our little ones have a story to tell but, at times, I find that the most unusual of stories often soften my heart and make me wish I had stopped what I was doing – no matter what overly important task I thought it was – and just take a few dedicated moments to really *listen* to my children. Maybe the spirit in the blue coat was helping me with my tasks while I was inside making breakfast to feed their physical body. Spirit has now, most certainly, given us spiritual food for thought.

"One's destination is never a place, but a new way of seeing things."

—Henry Miller
(1891-1980)

15. Across the Miles

When Xara was just seven weeks old we made a quick trip to Texas to visit with my angelic grandmother before she passed to spirit. It was really hot when we stepped off the airplane in Houston. Summer in Texas and I began to instantly melt. It was extremely humid and the 20 hour trip from England just seemed to have no end. To top it off I had carried Xara the whole way in my arms. I was completely - utterly - exhausted. We drove two more hours from the international airport to the little town I grew up in, Port Lavaca, arriving at my parent's home finally.

The next day we had planned to go over to the nursing home to see "Mamaw". She had been my most precious – other mother – all growing up. I loved her so much that even today it brings a tear to my eyes when I think of her and how long she's been gone. There is a void in my life that no one can fill and perhaps I really shouldn't think that anyone ever could. Maybe that's how all children feel about their grandmothers? Anyway, we went over to see her and on the way Mom was telling me that Mamaw wasn't quite herself anymore. I thought that was a silly thing to say but, I had been gone for three years and was not prepared for Mamaw to be just a 'little different'. Mamaw was always the same. Always. I was quite proud to be taking my lovely Xara to meet my even lovelier grandma. I couldn't wait to see her and I was a little disappointed when there were other family members already at the nursing home when we arrived. I had wanted to keep Mamaw all to myself. I wanted to just sit and talk to her like we used to do. I wanted to show off Xara and just sit and – be – with Mamaw. That's what we used to do when I was all growing up. And even after I grew up and left home I would still go to her house and sit and talk to her. We would talk about nothing really. I still remember her laugh and those shining eyes. You could say anything and she would laugh. I can't remember having heard her say a cross word about another living soul as long as I can recall. She was just the best person I ever – ever knew. And, I wasn't happy to have all these other people in the room taking up my time after I had flown 5000 miles to be with her.

After a short while I could see what Mom was talking about on the drive over to the nursing home. Mamaw didn't laugh any-more. She wasn't more serious – she was just a little.......lost looking. I tried joking with her in a silly way like I used to that always made her laugh but this time she didn't laugh. I used to joke with her about sitting in her dressing gown and say, "Look at you – you hussy." She would laugh and grin at me knowing I was kidding with her. This time she looked back at me and said, "I'm no hussy." She didn't remember people – I wondered if she knew who I was? She seemed to be put out with all the people in the room and when I left that day I knew I would not see her again on this side of life. I kissed her and told her I would come back to see her again before I left for England. She nodded as if she either didn't hear me or didn't care – maybe she just really didn't know me. I kissed her before we left and can still remember that smell that was uniquely my own Mamaw. It wasn't the smell of food or perfume – it was what I can only describe as - love.

We left the nursing home and I asked Mom to take me to the florist. I ordered the flowers for Mamaw's funeral as I knew it was all I had left that I could do for her. I would not be able to come back to her funeral with such a small baby in tow.

This had been a very hard trip for me – in more ways than one.

The very next day Xara and I made the long trip back to England. Once again, with Xara in my arms, carrying her through first one airport and then the next until we finally reached our home. I was relieved when we disembarked the airplane and the cool English air hit me in the face. It was nice to be home and even better to sleep in my own bed that night. I continued to phone Mom and check on Mamaw's progress each day. Each call found her slipping a little farther away from us.

A few weeks later, one night in August, I went to bed and I was woke up in the night by Mamaw standing next to the bed. The song playing in my head was one of Ronin Keating's at the time. It was playing, "If tomorrow never comes, will she know how much I loved her?" I knew my treasured grandma had passed from this life even before the phone rang the next morning. Ajaz answered the phone and said, "Yes, she already knows." He handed me the phone and it was Mom telling me that Mamaw had passed at exactly that some time she had been with me in the night. She came to say goodbye. And yes Mamaw, I know how much you love me.

That wasn't the last time I saw Mamaw either – I mean after she passed away. When Xara was a baby she used to sleep in our bed – between Ajaz and me. Since she was awake every two hours anyway it was just the most convenient place for me to tend to her. As I said previously, I am a very light sleeper. Somehow, even when I am supposedly asleep, I can still sense what is going on in the room around me. So, this one night, when Xara was in the middle of our bed – I was laying on my side facing her and at this point I had either moved down in the bed or Xara had moved up – whichever - it doesn't matter but, our heads were next to each other in the bed and separated by a matter of inches. I sensed someone in the room and opened my eyes – something caught the corner of my eye up above the bed! I saw a full spirit arm with a hand coming down from above the bed and reaching, lovingly, toward Xara's sleeping face. A heavenly hand was extending a loving brush across her cheek. It was the familiar aged hand of Mamaw. I just *knew* it was her. Those same familiar fingers I had watched crochet a million bedspreads – can a billion jars of pickled cucumbers – stir a zillion pots of bubbling stews. Mamaw reached across the heavens and stroked Xara's face as she lay there asleep beside me. Once again I was reminded - we are never forgotten. We are never alone.

"Ask and it will be given to you, seek and you will find, knock and the door will be opened."

The Bible
(Matthew 7:7)

16. Spirit Doctors

I know there are times in everyone's life when they feel so let down by either the medical world or perhaps they aren't very happy with the way a certain treatment is going for them that they cry out to the heavens for assistance. I can honestly say I've been there too. When Xara was only six months old we went to my niece's wedding in London. Of course, it was cold and raining on this particular weekend in November but we were all excited about the wedding reception so we made the most of it. I'm sure it was because of the weather and all the nasty tummy bugs going around that Xara came down with a virus that weekend and I will never forget it. Her vomiting and diarrhea lasted four months. Just as her symptoms would get a little better we would start the whole episode all over again. I took her to see the doctor many times and she was given several rounds of antibiotics. Finally, after about the first three months of going back and forth to the doctor and watching my poor daughter suffering I asked to be referred to a Consultant Pediatrician. As we waited for the referral to come through I decided I would try to take things into my own hands. It was at this time that I became very interested in Reiki healing. I know that we are all made up of energy and when we learn how to work more closely with it miracles can truly happen. I thought it was a natural thing for me to become interested in along with all my spirit work so, true to form, I dived right in and booked myself on a Reiki 1 class quickly followed by the rest of the classes as well as completing my Reiki Master Teacher level! I definitely need to work on developing more patience.

One night after I had finished putting Xara to bed and still quite aware that she was awake every few hours, I laid down on the bed thinking I would take a nap and still be near if she needed me. As I laid there I was sending Xara distance Reiki and I was instinctively tuning into the spirit world. I was also asking Spirit to send the help that Xara needed to get better and it was just then that I could feel someone walk into the room. I opened my eyes and I watched a lady in spirit come walking up to Xara's baby bed while holding a small silver tray. This Spirit nurse was dressed in the black and white nurses' uniform from the Victorian times complete with white apron and a hat neatly pinned on the top of her hair which was pulled up on her head in a bun. As she reached over into Xara's bed she patted her on the back and as she did the spirit nurse gently faded away out of my sight. I was so pleased to have been allowed to witness this interaction from the spirit world and I just knew Xara would soon be getting well.

Within a few days we got our referral appointment to take Xara to see the Consultant Pediatrician. It had taken so much effort to get the appointment I decided I would still keep the appointment which was in just a few days' time. Of course you can already guess by the time we did attend the appointment Xara was completely well and I felt a bit embarrassed to be wasting this important Dr.'s time. We went over her torturous list of recurring symptoms anyway and the Dr. said it was normal for this sort of an infection to "right itself" in about four months' time. He could say what he wanted but I already knew the truth of her miraculous recovery. Spirit had intervened to help stop the suffering of this poor precious child and I was so very grateful for their assistance.

That's not the only time I am aware of having a visit from a Spirit Doctor. Several years ago I had a small spot on my wrist begin to get larger and darker. At first it started out looking like a freckle and when it had reached the size of a pea and was growing up out of my wrist as well as in circumference I began to get a bit concerned. Having grown up in Texas I am well aware of the warning signs for skin cancer so I went down to my local Dr. to get her opinion. She examined my wrist and had a good look at the raised dark spot on my wrist. Although she said she wasn't very concerned with it she still offered me a referral to see a dermatologist and get his expert opinion. I happily accepted her offer and, once again, waited for the referral letter to be processed.

That night I went to bed really worrying about this raised dark spot on my wrist. I had been looking at it for many days and I was sure it was growing exponentially every hour! With this worry on my mind and trying to settle down for the night I began to say my nightly prayers. I included all the normal please and thank-you's that are contained in any worthy nightly offering but I went one step further that night. Since I had witnessed a spirit nurse in the past I asked if Spirit would please send me a Spirit Doctor to check and heal the skin cancer I was sure was growing heartily on my wrist. As my physical body fell into a deep sleep I was consciously aware of being in the Spirit world. After all these years I can tell the difference in several kinds of sleep time occurrences. These occurrences all have a very distinct 'feel' to them. There is the normal type thing we call a 'dream'. Then there is the realization of being in the spirit world as well as the understanding of being in another dimension of space and time. As I fell asleep I was very much aware I was in the spirit world. I was in a very bright white room and in the spirit world everything seems so full of a pure white light – and alive. You're surrounded by white energy and even the air seems to be alive and bright white. As I stood in this white room or space I was aware of a doctor with two nurses who came walking toward me. They were wearing white coats and as the doctor came up to me he asked to see my wrist. I held out my arm and gently tilted my left wrist clockwise so he could have a good look at the dark growth off on one side. The doctor reached into his pocket and produced a cream for me to rub on the spot. The cream had the look and feel of crushed diamonds. It was glistening and very abrasive with what I thought were big chunks of diamonds it in! He told me to continue rubbing the cream in a circular motion and then he and the nurses turned and walked out of the room. I sat there just looking at the cream glistening all over this dark spot and then something amazing happened! It was like I had zoomed in vision and I could see little dark bugs come to life under the cream and start scattering for dear life. These dark little 'bugs' were dropping off my wrist in a frenzy. It was the most amazing thing to watch and I am quite sure I will never forget seeing this. So, as the last few 'bugs' were falling off my wrist the doctor came back into the room to have a look at the results. I held up my wrist to show him that there was one bug still implanted directly in the middle of the dark spot. The doctor reached over with his fingers firmly grasping the last bug which now appeared to look like a small tick embedded in my wrist. With one firm quick action the doctor pulled the last bug out of the dark spot on my wrist and I actually felt a little pinching sensation as he did this. I actually felt the pain of him removing that last invader.

Now, here's the good part. Of course I woke up out of that 'dream' and looked at my wrist to see if the dark spot was gone. It remained but within one week of having that experience in the spirit world the dark spot completely disappeared off my wrist. I was so glad I had been telling my friend in the office while this was all happening. Shell is my witness if I ever need one but I am sure that spirit have helped me more than just those two occasions I am able to share with you now.

This is a slightly different story but still involves the help of a type of Spirit doctor. I went to visit a friend recently that hasn't been well as she had broken her wrist. While I was there I offered to do a Reiki treatment on her to which she happily accepted. Even though I am a Reiki Master it had been several years since I had given anyone, except the kids, a Reiki treatment. My friend, Pauline, and I finished off our tea and went up to her treatment room. Pauline is a very gifted healer on many levels and has her own treatment room which she does many therapies out of. I felt privileged to be allowed to use her sacred space as well as being allowed to conduct a treatment on her too. This may have been the first time I had ever offered to do a healing on her as she is normally the one sending healing to everyone else.

Moments into beginning the treatment a Zen Master showed up to assist in her session. He was dressed in orange robes and as he hit his staff on the ground he shouted, "HO!" and lightening shot out of the staff and hit me causing me to begin to sweat profusely! Three times he repeated the sequence shouting, "HO!" each time. I continued the treatment moving all around my friend picking up information along the way as the energy flowed. The room seemed to get hotter and hotter and even Pauline commented on how the room had heated up while I was working on her.

We got to the end of the treatment and I told her everything I had picked up as well as a totem animal that was in the room too. We were both guessing what this Zen Master might have been saying when he was shouting 'Ho' at me and I told Pauline I would try to look it up later. Arriving home I got right on the computer and tried to find out what 'HO' means and was as surprised as usual by spirit when I found out it is a Japanese mantra for "Open the channel." I guess this Zen Master thought he would help me in channeling the much needed healing energy to my friend's broken wrist. It took me a while to stop sweating!

So, remember, if you are in need of any kind of assistance you now have the knowledge of spirit doctors and nurses you can also call on for help. Don't forget to say please – and thank you!

"Everything has already been decided. It was known long ago what each person would be.
So there's no use arguing with God about your destiny."

—The Bible
Ecclesiastes 6:10

17. Seven Sacred Symbol Assignment

One morning in March, 2009 I woke up and spirit was there as they are many times. It's not unusual to have a whole parade going on at times. In the day or during the night they come in – they go out. It's nothing new or unexpected. So, this one particular spring morning I could see the sun shining around the edges of the closed curtain. Through the stillness in the room I heard a voice say to me, "You will be working with seven sacred symbols." I lay there, motionless, waiting for more information. I needed Spirit to tell me what these symbols were – where to find them and, most importantly, what to do with the symbols when I *had* found them. But, that's all the voice said and I was left to try to figure out the rest for myself, or so I thought.

Having been aware of Spirit since I was a child I knew that this brief message was the first time they had ever made an 'announcement' to me. A life spent working with Spirit has taught me one thing is certain – when Spirit talks – I listen.

As I was not an artist at that time what was to occur over the next 10 months really amazed me. I know deep in my being that the gifts of psychic mediumship I was born with are really all of our natural state of being whether we acknowledge and use them or not. I know when information is flowing and I have a 'good connection'. Perhaps the whole journey up to this point was preparing me for what would happen next. Perhaps I had needed to develop enough trust and experience to bring through the information in the form of visual mnemonics and associated messages that would be flowing through me to the physical world.Each painting emits a vibration which may be used in meditation or contemplation. Symbols are keys. Keys open doorways – sometimes to you and sometimes to other (higher) dimensions. Only the observer can determine which key is most beneficial at a particular point in their sacred journey.

I fully understand that one of the symbols is very controversial but keep in mind that this is not a project I have assembled. It is an *assignment* I have dutifully been bringing to life. There are times when being of service you don't have the luxury of asking your Boss, "Why?" You just do it.

So, I spent the next few weeks wondering each day when or where I was to find these 'sacred symbols' the spirit at the end of my bed spoke to me about. I've said it before and I will say it again – I can be a bit thick sometimes. Maybe I should be kind to myself and say I am a bit naïve and not thick. Sometimes I have to let new ideas sink in and let them bubble away within my being and then see what comes back up to the surface as my understanding of the situation. Sometimes things aren't immediately clear to me. I think it might be my easy going attitude and knowing that the right things come at the right time and in the right way. I allow the flow to continue for my highest good and then I just expect it in my experience.

I had purchased a large assortment of artist's materials for my daughter, Xara, as she is very creative. I also got drawing pads and markers for Rocco and Marcus too. No one gets left out at our house whether they want to or not. I am happy if you just try something new. If you don't like it then we go on to something else and see if you excel at that instead. So, we were on to art supplies at this particular juncture in our house. I was in the living room tidying away some of the pads and pencils when I decided I needed to just sit down for a minute and have a little break. The pad of paper was on my lap with a fresh clean page exposed and the pencil was loosely in my dominant hand. As I sat there relaxing I thought to myself that I wished I was a good artist. As I put the pencil on the paper I began to draw a big circle. The pencil felt encouraged I guess because after about 15 minutes there was a fully drawn sketch of a woman. I couldn't believe what I was seeing! I sent out the thought in my head to the woman in the sketch, "Someone so beautiful must have a name!" And the lady in the sketch replied, "My name is Maya. I come to awaken the sleeping eye."

I was amazed! Xara walked into the living room where I was and I said, "Hey look at this!"She smiled and said, "That's good. You can draw good Mummy! Hey, that's not fair – I'm the one who's supposed to be learning to draw – not you."

I replied, "I can't believe I've just drawn this either, Xara. I don't know how to draw."

She just smiled at me and said, "It's pretty good for someone who can't draw!" and she went about her business as before not fully taking in what I was trying to tell her.

I took the sketch into the kitchen and put it on the counter still wondering what had just happened. Ajaz came walking in and I quickly picked up the sketch and showed it to him. "Look at what I just drew." This man I had been with for the last 13 years looked at it and said, "I didn't know you could draw." I quickly replied, "No, I can't!"He just looked at me and then the sketch and made a sort of smiley surprised face. It was yet again something unusual going on in our house. He's learned to just go with the flow over the course of the years. That's one of the things I love about Ajaz. I can just be me and I don't have to worry about being ridiculed or having to hide my gifts. He actually encourages me and supports me in everything I take on. I look forward to sharing new developments with him and getting his feedback as to how to proceed. He's the logical thinker in our house. I live in my spirit and he lives in the world. Together we make a whole person.

Maya with Diamonds

Maya is the Goddess of Illusion who helps us to see through the veil of illusion to what is real. There are those today who also understand the importance of the DIAMONDS and their re-emergence in our history today. In Karen French's book, *Gateway to the Heaven's,* Karen refers to the diamond as being based on the Triangular Grid of Being which arises from the trinity of the human being (mind, body, spirit). It is the 'mind' element which unites the other two elements (body & spirit) and allows us to transcend the time/space problem we encounter. It is OUR own mind which separates us from the rest of the Universe. The DIAMOND is here to awaken that part of our mind which allows us to perceive what we have been overlooking - we are not alone. The Diamond is a tool for magnifying and tuning. And it is here now to tune our mind to perceive that which has been beyond our reality. Maya will now help us to move beyond illusion into a new reality with the help of the DIAMONDS.

The sketch of Maya with Diamonds (from the front room) came in after I had actually started painting the first two symbols. As well as buying sketch pads and pencils I had purchased a few canvases and some acrylic paints for Xara to doodle about with. I wanted her to have all the items she needed to fully explore the world of artistry and her own creativity. Little did I know that spirit was leading me by my children to my own destiny. While cleaning away her paints one day in the conservatory I looked at a fresh white canvas which was left on the window ledge in the conservatory window. The paints where nearby so I picked some up and squeeze out a few prime colors on the palate. I dipped the brush into one color and then then next allowing them to arrange on the canvas in quite a natural flow. I was amazed, once again, at the beauty that arranged itself on the canvas. I was just the instrument for the orchestra that played upon the canvas. When it was all finished I backed up and had a nice long look at what had just appeared in front of me. Then in one open spot on the canvas Spirit showed me an OM symbol, so that's what I put next and it was finished.

Om – The Creation

Om (Aum) is thought to be the sound (vibration) which the Great Creator spoke to create the Universe. It was the first divine utterance in a vast void. "Om" has its roots deeply implanted in the Cosmic Code of Creation. All other sounds and all languages were created from the divine sound of OM which is represented by this Golden Sanskrit Symbol which looks like the number 3 with other swirly bits attached.

Om is re-birthing at this time to help each of us in the CREATION process as there are those of us who actively working to raise the consciousness of this planet. By bringing OM into your existence you can truly create anything your heart desires. It literally helps you to start over and to kick start new projects or breathe life into old ones!

Tetra-gammadion: The next symbol was shown to me one morning as I got dressed. As I sat at my dressing table in the guest room a white canvas appeared before me. I thought, "Oh good here comes the next symbol." I sat and watched in anticipation. I was very impatient and asked, "What color goes on this canvas?" With that request the canvas turned black. Not an ominous foreboding sort of black but, a very deep universe sort of black if you can understand what I mean. It had a very expansive sort of feel to it as though it went on forever. I sat and watch. Again impatient I asked, "What goes on this beautiful black backdrop?" With that request I could see something appear very small in the very center of the canvas and begin to grow. I watch it grow until the image filled the entire canvas and when I saw what it was I just said, "No - way." First in a whisper, "no- way" and then a little louder, "no-way" and then finally in my normal voice as I looked at what had appeared, "No way – you can't ask me to do this one!"

I was, of course, speaking to spirit. I am an American and this symbol only meant one thing to me. My Granddad was in World War II so you can imagine what was running through my mind when I was shown what I could only identify, at the time, as a swastika. I let it sink in but only briefly because then I immediately had the realization that if I had been having some ego trip up to this point and making up all these symbols out

of some fairy tale in my head – there is "no-way" I would have
ever in a million years used this one! I knew at that moment that
Spirit really was giving me something unique that I was being
asked to assemble and bring together for a special purpose. And,
this is when I realized that; once again I would do as Spirit asked
of me and bring this symbol through too. Sometimes when you
work for Spirit you don't have the luxury of telling your Boss,
"No thank you." You just do it. And that's what I have done.

Of course I began looking up this symbol to find out
everything I could about it. How could I bring this back out into
public view and not know very much about it? I have come to
know that the Tetra-gammadion is the oldest and most powerful
symbol we know of. This is a very auspicious symbol which can
be traced back over 5000 years. It is still a much honored symbol
in many ancient religions today too having only been desecrated
when Hitler adopted its use for his own insignia. Not only did
Hitler murder an estimated 11 million people of varying race,
creed, color and sexual orientation, he also desecrated this
sacred symbol and caused its association to be held in such
abhorrent, gruesome company that this image is still outlawed
in Germany today.

Hitler did not have this symbol created for him as a proud
family would do with a coat of arms or a family crest. He adopted a
symbol which was already in use and much revered with ancient
occult connections. He tried to tap into the symbol and use it
for his own devices. The tetra-gammadion can be used for great
good or great evil. When used for evil it will literally tear apart
the person or the cause it is being used for. This did eventually
happen to Hitler. Unfortunately, the tetra-gammadion has
not recovered to the stature it once enjoyed prior to its cursed
connections with the 3rd Reich.

This sacred symbol is thought to be the symbolic
representation of the name of God or Yahweh. Perhaps thinking
he could tap into the power of God for his own purposes; Hitler

used this symbol in his campaign of terror which lasted six years and one day. This length of time equates to 2,191 days or the number 13. Spiritually speaking this is an important number. In the Jewish tradition it is among the holiest of numbers because it is associated with God. Meaning, there were twelve tribes of Israel and Israel itself being number thirteen. Number thirteen relates to the transcendent dimension of Godliness. This transcendence allows us to infuse spirituality into the physical world which in turn leads us back to the symbol, the tetra gammadion or swastika. This must have been Hitler's thinking at the time of adopting this powerful most sacred symbol as his own. I do not in any way mean to assume that I am a Jewish scholar and this is a far too deep subject for me but, it is well worth having a look at and gaining a deeper knowledge of the origins of this sacred symbol.

The tetra-gammadion is rebirthing in a positive way at this time. You may have noticed that the symbol spins in either the right or left direction. A right facing symbol emits the vibration of universal peace and universal evolution. A left spinning symbol is 'involution' which allows for the function of 'evolution' to occur. Involution and Evolution create balance. Involution is the act of involvement. It is involving evolution but this time on a universal scale. This time emitting the vibration of universal peace and allowing us to come into alignment to be able to rejoin the rest of the universe in a peaceful way. I like that interpretation a lot better than the past association it was being strangled with.

< I have intentionally not inserted the Tetra-gammadion picture here as I do not wish to offend anyone who is not ready for this image. You may see it on my website. This image is still outlawed in Germany.>

Eye of Consciousness: The fourth symbol was also channeled over the course of eight hours on one fine sunny summer day as my children played in the garden. The children would pop into the conservatory occasionally to see how things were developing and then toddle off to play in the sun again. *The Eye of Consciousness* was coming through in more than one way that day.

The Eye of Consciousness

The EYE is literally the symbol of conscious awareness. We see what we perceive to be 'reality' through our eyes. The awakening consciousness of our planet is depicted here. Absolutely everything is connected. There is just no getting around it. As our planet's consciousness awakens to a higher level we will all begin to see a new reality. The all seeing eye of the Creator is upon us. It is my personal belief that the 'tunnel of light' people talk about going through to pass to the other side is actually the process of us going back into Source - entering through his eye as we have never left his sight.

Puja - The Unity: The fifth painting seemed to be the hardest and take the longest. I looked at a blank canvas for many weeks petitioning Spirit to *just show me what to do*. The painting which Spirit called 'Puja' was full of messages and at one point I had a door of white light open in my conservatory and many Ascended Masters came walking through the light and vanished *into* the painting. I was left feeling very humble that day indeed.

Puja – The Unity

The Unity contains the cosmic energy of the Chohans of each of the 7 rays. It was actually St. Germaine who came through to help me get this painting going, hence the lilac background.

So you can see how this painting encapsulates so much energy with all these ascended masters included! Wisdom, Patience, Love, Understanding, Compassion, Protection, Upliftment, Healing, Transformation, Transmutation and so many many more energies. Far too many to list here exhaustively. These Ascended Masters are working together in an effort to unify all their energies for the highest good of all of I Am and to assist in our ascension process.

The night before I was to begin receiving this information I was turning the bed down in the guest room and I heard spirit say to me, "Carpathia." I stopped to listen for more but there was nothing more forthcoming. Well, I had only ever heard that once before in the Ghostbuster movies. I thought for a moment, "What would Spirit be trying to tell me with that one word?"

I did not know but I did know that it would probably become apparent soon.

The very next day (how's that for quick?) I did get the information coming through to begin this painting. And it was brought through by someone in Spirit calling themself "Chohan of the 7th Ray". That's all he said and you can already guess I didn't know what a Chohan was or what this term meant. I thanked spirit and later I googled 'Chohan of the 7th Ray'. Indeed it was Saint Germaine who is known as the Chohan (master) of the 7th Ray of light and who has his earthly retreat in the Carpathian Mountains no less! So, his energy had started coming through the night before gently.

Another time I was stuck as to what to do next. I had painted as far as spirit had led me and I just needed some more guidance. So, I asked spirit for help. Then, I waited. I waited a few days and then a few days more. It turned into a few weeks. As I cooked dinner one night I kept looking at the partially finished painting out in the conservatory. I told myself that I obviously needed to do more than just ask this time. So I made a plan that I kicked into action a bit later that evening. As I sat meditating in front of the painting, when all of the family had calmed down, I decided to call on Saint Germaine as he had brought me the information to start the painting off when I had waited and waited in the beginning for this image.

"May I speak to Saint Germaine please?" I quietly said.

Almost immediately a being of light appeared. In front of me was not Saint Germaine but someone calling himself Serapis Bey. (I had not heard that name before either.) He was dressed all in white clothes – with white boots and a large white turban sort of head gear. Now, one would think when you have an ascended master in front of you that you would be quite happy - right? Well, I said, "Thank you but may I please speak to Saint Germaine?"

Serapis Bey was standing just to the right of the painting and he raised his arm in the direction of the painting - like presenters on stage do when they are introducing others to come out. As he raised his arm a door of white light opened over on the left of the painting and a whole cast of Ascended Masters came walking through. I saw each of them walk past the painting and when they got to the center of it they each disappeared as if they were walking INTO the painting. As the last ascended master disappeared - so did Serapis Bey. He just turned and walked right into the painting

It was as if he was telling me "Look - call one or call all - we are here and are ready to assist."

I just sat there in the silence and wondered what to expect next? I felt very humbled that day and every day since. In reading I have since found out that Serapis Bey is the Chohan who is the teacher to the path of ascension. I think it's very appropriate that he would sort of be the leader of the pack on this occasion. I thanked Spirit for their visit and asked that I be able to learn what it was that I am to do with all of this information that I was being given. I still had no idea what was to come but I was, and am, always happy to assist Spirit with whatever I am asked to do.

The next day, I was working on the painting and spirit said one more word to me - 'Puja'. I didn't know what it meant but I did know that when I hear something (especially when I don't know what it means) that it is bound to mean SOMETHING... so I thanked spirit, wrote it down and after putting the children to bed, googled it.Once again I have been totally amazed at the confirmation Spirit gives to me over and over again. Basically, if you're not familiar with the term 'puja' as I wasn't, it means an object which it is believed to contain the cosmic energy or spiritual energy of divinity and is a means of contacting Divine Spirit. I also wondered if that was the message all the Masters where trying to tell me as each one walked into the painting? Since I did not know immediately, they had to tell me the word to google the next day. (They know I like to research!)

A few years later I felt compelled to send a poster size copy of this painting to John of God in Brazil. So, that's what I did. I don't know exactly why but, I am sure one day I will find out. (Update: After writing that I have been given the information from someone who travels to see John of God of Brazil that he has healing triangles painted on several walls in his complex. They are said to be healing symbols which connect you with the Divine. If you place your head up to the triangle and make your request I am told there have been some miraculous healings come through.)

Peacock Feather - The Avatar: The sixth painting was a flash of insight but took me several weeks of research to fully understand the depth of meanings involved in a peacock feather. Well, even now I can't really say I fully understand all of the complexities of this symbol.

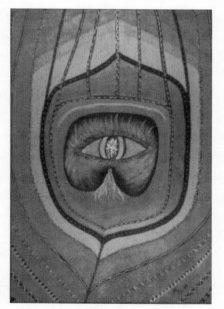

Peacock Feather – The Avatar

Peacock Feather - The Symbol of the Avatar

An Avatar is a divine being who has come into a physical embodiment to assist on the physical plane. It is our ego which assumes that the Avatar is only here to assist humanity. This Divine Being has already walked this Earth plane, and most probably other planes of existence, many many times and has undergone a vast amount of spiritual growth in order to ascend to the state of divinity in which it currently resides. It is their knowledge of the Divine Creator which enables them to have the LOVE necessary to want to come back once again in a selfless act of service to assist those still searching on their spiritual path.

The peacock feather is said to have been worn in the hair of the first Sai Baba who is a respected and adored holy man in India. It is said that Sai Baba is an avatar. The peacock feather is also called the 1000 eyes of God and are said to carry spiritual healing abilities to anyone wishing to connect to the Universal Healing Energy which is available to anyone who will seek it.

The Peacock is also viewed as the modern day version of the Phoenix. It is said the Peacock can help you on your spiritual path - just like the avatar - as it helps boost your self-esteem and helps you to show your true colours.

The peacock feather is a symbol of spirituality, healing, resurrection, immortality, faith, vision, glory, royalty, guidance, protection and watchfulness. The list of positive attributes seems to be endless.

Peacock feathers are as individual to a peacock as our own fingerprints are to each of us. Colors not only add to the beauty in life, they also have their own vibrations and send out a tangible signal which can be felt by many sensitives.

The colors used in this painting are:

Turquois - giving protection to the traveller... in this case it is the spiritual journey.

Green - used for Universal Harmony and Love - green sends out a strong balancing signal.

Yellow - intelligence and creativity - self-confidence, optimism, emotionally strengthens and uplifts

Pink - represents the feminine ability to nurture, love, encourage and uplift others. Pink truly is a compassionate colour.

Gold - illumination, love, compassion, wisdom

Black - spiritual and physical healing properties, black absorbs light, protection

There are other uses and attributes to color as well as many associated stones which may be used in similar ways.

The black lines of the peacock feather represent the lonely roads we each journey on our spiritual paths to enlightenment. The hardest journey of all is in awakening to the fact that we are never really ever alone at all. We are on the journey from separation back to Oneness. The gold patterns represent the patterns of The All That Is as He/She tries to guide our path. Each golden path is touched with the struggle with duality - the light and the dark. On one path there is a prayer written in Angelic text which says:

Namaste,

Giving thanks to God we call out to you for help.

Hear our prayers for guidance and assistance in all issues meant for our highest good.

May the eternal light of love, peace, joy, wisdom and compassion guide our ascension.

In the name of All That Is,

Amen (Om)

Then in the center we have the all seeing eye of God. There is that vision of who we are and who we wish to become. There is the knowledge that we are being watched, guided and indeed have spirit close enough at any point in our journey to just look up and make eye contact. How do you view those around you? There are avatars walking unaware to you - in your everyday life. Open your eyes. Wake up. Be a modern day Avatar. Even if you think you walk alone; you do not. Share your gifts with each other. Love each other. Help each other. These gifts are given to you and it is your duty to share them. Share the Avatar in YOU.

The Master's Staff: The seventh painting occurred in a brilliant vision. I was in a room full of living white light. It was the whitest of whites I have ever seen and even the air seemed to be alive. The next day I was trying to sketch what I had been shown so I wouldn't forget any of it (like that's going to ever happen!)

Master's Staff

As we move into these very quickly changing times we are reminded that we are never alone.

The Master still guides all who will follow. When I was given this symbol I was shown a room all full of white light. It was the 'whitest of whites' I have ever seen - but never in the physical world. The whole room was full of white flowing energy and there was a man in the center of the room. This man had flowing white robes of energy all swirling around him. He was walking toward the center of the room which means that his back was to me so all I could see in the midst of this white room was the top of his head and the staff he carried.

This image consumed me all that night until the next day. I sat down to try and sketch what I had been given so I would not forget any of it. As I sat there sketching I heard spirit say, "You were allowed to see The Master." And that's all they said.

It has been very difficult trying to paint an all-white picture!! But Spirit has guided me and I have done the very best I could do.

The Staff is Creator's ultimate symbol of absolute authority to create great change! It has been present since the Garden of Eden and has been handed down through time and tribes with God's authority to rule. The Torah says that the original staff was made of Sapphire and weighed 1300 pounds. It took someone with God's help to even be able to carry it around!

The Staff was used by Moses to invoke most of the 10 plagues and then it was used again by Moses to part the Red Sea. The Staff is also a symbol for the Tree of Life and also refers to the Sephir`ot which is the 10 attributes in Kabbalah in which God reveals himself and is constantly creating the physical dimension and the higher spiritual (metaphysical) dimensions. The Staff is a means of channelling a higher creative life-force.'The Master's Staff' is the Creator's reminder that He has always remained in contact with us and that by His absolute authority we are able to channel the means to create change in our lives.

"Children are the bridge to heaven."

—Persian Proverb

18. One Eyed Girl

I was asleep one night and having the most vivid dream I have had in a very long time! It was really in depth and I was trying to pay very close attention to the possible meaning I could surmise from it. Just then (physically back in the room in my bed) I could feel what I thought was one of the children tapping me from my side of the bed. I could feel someone tapping my hand which was secured under the bed covers and being held up to my cold nose. Well, it is England and I seem to always have a cold nose at night! So, I sleep with my hand sort of covering my nose so my warm breath keeps my nose kind of defrosted. Anyway, judging by the quick tapping on my hand I could tell that one of my children really wanted me to wake up. I was a little in between being asleep and awake but I could feel them tap my hand once more through the covers.

As I was now fully awake I began to raise my hand – and the cover over the top of it – so I could have a look at which of my three little ones was in such need of assistance. As I got the cover raised far enough that I could *almost* see who was standing there – the tap, tap, tap on my hand went once again. I was a little annoyed if I am truthful. I threw the cover up to interrogate which ever child was unfortunate enough to have waked the sleeping bear and - no one was there.

I thought to myself – this is spirit waking me up again. What could be so important? They had never in my whole life – ever – tapped me! Well maybe I can't say that as I have had a regular visitor over the last 25 years slap my feet so hard it wakes me up with a startle every time it happens. I still don't know why they do it but I would love to find out! Why go to all that trouble to build up the energy needed for such a hard 'whop!' and then not take the time to communicate any farther?

Back to the story – I had just had someone tapping on my hand until it woke me completely awake – and then I had one more tap, tap when I was awake just for good measure. They obviously wanted me to understand that I had not been dreaming the whole thing. We do tend to rationalize some of these 'events' away far too often I think. Wondering what was so important I had begun running a checklist through my head.

Was someone trying to break into the house and spirit was warning me? I didn't think so as we have perimeter alarms and none of them had went off. When those are activated the flood lights pop on outside and an alarm sounds inside the house. It only takes one shrill beeeep and I'm awake without spirit prompting me anyway. That wasn't it.

Was everything okay with my sleeping kids? I listened with my bionic mom's ears down the hall. Not a sound. So I sat up in bed and tilted my head towards the open doorway as if doing that would help me hear better. Not a thing – no crying – no house noises – nothing. I sat up in bed trying to understand what spirit wanted me to wake up for? Just as I sat fully up in the bed with my feet dangling over the side, starting to doubt myself that anything really had tapped me, something happened. My legs – and only my legs – were covered in goose bumps! This is what happens when the energy of a spirit gets close enough to rub up against your aura – your energy. Someone was still standing there waiting for me! They really were trying to get my attention for some reason. I decided to go have a look at the children just to make sure everything was really okay.

I walked down the hall to the other end of the house still listening as I quietly crept. It was night, for goodness sakes, and I had reverted to being ten years old again. The hall light downstairs, standing guard by the front door, shined through the open slats on the stairs so at the very least it wasn't pitch black where I was as I moved closer to the kids room. I slowly opened the door latch and went in. Two sleeping boys safe in their beds – as I pretty much thought they would be. Then a quick glance in Xara's room proved that the perimeter alarms were indeed working properly. I closed her door and stood in the hall, alone, for a moment to think.

I continued running my checklist of possible things to consider as 'emergency reasons' to need to be tap, tap, tapped awake in the middle of the night. Was someone back home trying to reach me? Had they been texting or phoning me and I didn't know because, although I leave my mobile phone on the bedside table, it's left in the 'silence' mode at night. As I stood there in the hall it occurred to me – I would have to go back into the bedroom to get my phone off the bedside table to check out this theory! The ten year old in me returned and as I crept back through the open door, into the blackened room, something occurred to me. Ajaz was asleep in the bed! I giggled a little as I thought how ridiculous I was being. It wasn't the first time I had dealings with spirit! I knew there was nothing to be afraid of! It's just normal that we sometimes get a little edgy when we aren't completely sure of what's going on. And, I wasn't completely sure! I retrieved my phone from the bedside table and immediately saw that no one had been trying to reach me *that* way.

Being completely, absolutely, positively, *awake* I decided to go downstairs. I would go ahead and check the rest of the house – just in case. Getting downstairs I turned off the internal burglar alarm. What I really needed was a spirit communicator and not this bleeping box on the wall. In this room – to the next – each room obviously clear. I made my way to the kitchen contemplating having a cup of tea. (Well I am in England and that's the cure for absolutely everything here! A cup 'o tea love?) When I had left the bedroom I had noticed the time on the digital clock next to the bed – 12:15am. Realizing this when I got to the kitchen I thought maybe a cup 'o tea might not be the best thing to help me get back to sleep shortly so I took out a piece of paper and decided to jot down what had just happened. I wanted to be clear on the matter when I got up the next morning. I quickly scribbled out the front and back of a piece of lined notebook paper. It doesn't take long at all when you are writing lightening fast as the words fly past your mind once more and out your clinched fist.

I sat there for a moment still trying to make sense of it all. Just then I thought I would really need to go back to bed but – that's where the....uh......ghost was! I looked at the clock above the kitchen door. It was 1:30am!! I had lost an hour sitting there and it had only taken me a couple of minutes to scribble out the notes on the paper. Where had I lost an hour?

I turned off the lights. Turned the alarm system back on and walked back up the stairs to our room. I must admit I walked a little slower than normal into the room and may have peeked around the door to....uh.....steady myself before going all the way back in. Ajaz was still there asleep in bed so the spirit obviously had no use of him! I walked back to my side of the bed sort of expecting to feel those goose bumps again as I met up with the waiting spirit. There was no one there so I went back to bed. I sent out my thoughts to try to communicate with this person but had nothing return to me. Assuming the event was over I resumed my nightly habit of pulling the covers up and covered my still freezing nose. Surprisingly I fell straight back to sleep.

I thought I had been asleep for awhile and was suddenly struck back awake by someone bashing me on the arm! Bash! Bash! Bash! Instinctively the covers flew back as I had the begeebers scared out of me this time! Only this time there was someone standing next to the bed! It was one of the twins – six year old Marcus. He was standing there crying and his whole body was shaking. He was obviously very disturbed and as he pointed to the open door sobbing he said, "Mummy there's a girl in my room. There's a girl in my room and she's only got one eye!" Well, you don't mess with a momma bear's cubs and so I got up and we started out the door and down the hall to the room he shares with his brother, Rocco. This has stopped being something amusing that I would have to figure out at a later date if I had time. It had gone directly to the front of the "To-Do" list.

I gave him a big hug and tried to calm him down but he was the most scared I have ever seen him. He wouldn't stop shaking and crying. I took him by the hand and assured him I would take care of it. Marcus seemed to believe me as he stopped crying and we went together down the hall clutching one another's hands for safety. Walking back into the darkened room, slightly lit by a nightlight in a far corner of the room, Marcus was looking all around as if to see if this one-eyed girl was still there. Rocco was tucked safely up in his bed sound asleep.

I helped Marcus back into his bed and asked, "Do you still see her?" He looked around again but didn't answer me. I continued, "Markie do you think you may have been dreaming or did you really see someone?" I wanted to propose another option to help sooth his obviously frazzled nerves.

Marcus pulled the cover up and wiped his nose with one crumpled corner of it. "I... she... she was here... I...think... well... I don't know." He was obviously still upset so I said, "Well, if she was here I think she is gone now. I don't see anyone now. I think you will be just fine to go back to sleep. Okay? And remember, Markie, even if you do see a spirit they can't do anything to you. They don't have a body like we do. Tell me what you remember to say when you are afraid?"

Searching his memory banks Marcus quickly recited, "I call on Archangel Michael to wrap me in his blue cloak of protection." With that he seemed to relax and I thought it was okay to leave him to go back to sleep. I reminded him to say his prayers and that anytime he did that God would send an extra angel to watch over him. He covered up his head (maybe his nose was cold too!) and so I left his room to return to my own.

I went back to bed and was nearly asleep when I heard the latch on his bedroom door open – a slow release and *click* as the door was opened. I waited a moment as I thought he would probably be running down the hall to me again crying. I lifted my head off the pillow to listen closer, but heard nothing. I couldn't figure out why he had opened the door but not come to see me so I got up and started back out of my room and down the hall. As I got far enough down the hall I could see that his bedroom door was still closed. Curious, I quietly went into his room so as to not wake him if he had indeed been able to get back to sleep.

His covers were still over his head but they seemed to be moving slightly. I reached down to move the cover so I could see his face. As I began to move the covers they quickly flew back and he was still there shaking and sobbing like before. I felt so bad for him and said, "Oh, Markie what's wrong now honey?"

He said sobbing, with tears and nose juice running down his face, "Mummy she's only got one eye. I keep asking God to take this pain out of my head but he won't take it. Why won't he take it away?"As he was saying he had a pain in his head he was actually holding his cupped palm over one of his right eye. I was aware that this one eyed girl had found out how to communicate with me – through my son. She was super imposing the pain of her injury on him to get a response out of me. I told Marcus, "You've seen Mummy clear the house before, right?" His interest peeked and he shook his head, "Y...yes." This statement seemed to calm him down a little. Perhaps it was the hope of getting this girl to leave him alone tonight.

If you don't know what it means to 'clear the house' as opposed to 'cleaning the house' then I will tell you. It's actually pretty similar now that I think about it. If you clean your physical house you will tidy up and clean away all the dirt. You get rid of all the nasty unclean stuff that clutters your home – your space – and you make your living area nice and clean. It's fresh and sparkling and alive feeling, isn't it? Well, when you 'clear the house' in the sense I was speaking about you do the same thing but on a spiritual level. You will clear out all the stagnant energy or you will clear away any entities that might be hanging around being – let's say – naughty. Some of them aren't really being naughty – they just need to be sent to God's light as they have become a little lost on their journey back home.

Marcus had seen me clear the house many times before. It usually occurs on a monthly basis at our home as we all seem to be a bit sensitive to our surroundings. This normally includes me lighting sage brush and walking in each room of the house – calling in the angels as I go and clearing out any negativity that might be lingering. Anyone who does this on a regular basis will probably develop their own style and use materials, sage brush, candles, incense or other items that suits their personal beliefs. I usually fill each room with God's Highest Light before leaving to move on to the next room. I have the feeling, looking back on the situation, that's what this one-eyed girl was waiting for. She was ready to go home and had seen the light in our house. That's what had attracted her to us that night and she wasn't leaving until we waved the magic wand and she could click her heels and go home. (Don't you just love the Wizard of Oz?)

I asked Marcus if he would like me to clear his room and he quickly agreed that he would. I walked to the first corner of his room (energy stagnates in corners) and I raised my hand making a clearing symbol and clearing the energy there. I moved on to the next corner and did the same thing. When I got to the third corner – the hair on my whole body stood up!! I knew she was standing there. It was time to send her home – all the way home. Some people call it Heaven. Some people just call it the Spirit World. It doesn't matter – she just needed some help getting there. I made the commands as I had been taught so many years ago, "I command you to go to God's Highest Light."

As I spoke these words I saw a brilliant light open up from the ceiling shining down into the room. It was a type of ladder for this spirit child to climb up to God's Light – our spiritual home. I watched the spirit of this little girl go up into the light. As soon as she had cleared the ceiling the light closed back up and the room seemed lighter. I went to the fourth corner of the room and cleared that space too.

Marcus seemed all better to have witnessed me clear the room. I told him she was gone for sure this time as I had watched her leave. She had gone to be with the angels in heaven. Marcus smiled and said the pain in his head was gone and whispered as he covered up his head to go back to bed, "Thank you Mummy. Good night. I love you."

I went back to bed and said a prayer for the little girl we had helped go home. I felt confident the events of the night had finally drawn to a close and that we wouldn't be having any more troubles for the rest of the night.

It was a couple of nights later and I had a dream. It was as clear as day this dream. The little one eyed girl had come back with a brief message for me. Her name was Elizabeth. She looked as though she was floating in water; her long golden hair was flowing all around and above her as though it was suspended in liquid. She was indeed missing one eye but she was not scary to me. She was a child who had died by an injury and yet she was smiling. She didn't want to tell me what it was and I had no feeling as to what had inflicted such a heavy injury on her as to take her life. Her only message was this, "The incredible human heart – paint it." Then I woke up. This small child had observed our family long enough to know you can control someone through their heart. Elizabeth was able to speak to me through pulling my heart strings. The love of my own children had helped me to understand that a little lost girl needed to go home to God's light; her spiritual home. I felt as though she was thanking me.

Our purpose in this life is quite clear to me. We are here to help each other. We each have special gifts, talents and ways that we can do just that – help. It doesn't matter if we help each other while we are here or in a different dimension of space and time. We all need help from time to time. It doesn't matter if you are a spirit *in* a body or *outside* of a body. If you need help then you look for it until you find it.

"Mother Mary seeks for those who approach her devoutly
and with reverence,
for such she loves, nourishes, and adopts as her children."

-Saint Bonaventure, Doctor of the Church
(1221 – 1274)

"Mother Mary Contemplating Unfinished Work" ©2013
Michelle Rathore

19. Mother Mary

I have had the very great honor of being visited by Mother Mary on two occasions. The first time I was overcome with an urge to go sit in our clear glass conservatory with my sketchpad and water colors while listening to some gentle music on the iPod. As I sat there at the long dining table which seats 12, relaxing and waiting for inspiration to come to me, I was impressed with the energy of Mother Mary. It was a very gentle feeling to begin with and as I was impressed with this information I began working with my sketchpad. I noticed the colors were very regal looking and I wasn't really sure what the design was all about but I just keep letting the energy flow and enjoyed the peaceful feeling that had come over me and continued to intensify. I had been sketching about ten or fifteen minutes when I became aware there was an energy coming toward me from up high above me and far beyond the physical glass walls of the conservatory. As I looked up, still in the light filled conservatory, I was aware of an enormous amount of angels that were coming down from the sky in what seemed like two rows with a very large empty space between them. They were glorious beings of Light that were indeterminately bright and yet you could make out their apparently human form. The two angels in front seemed to be carrying some sort of rod with each of them

which was held tight and out in front of them as though in a protective stance. Then, very quickly, Mother Mary descended from
the midst of all these angelic beings right into the big empty space
that had been left open for her. I was overcome with a feeling of
bliss and awe all at the same time. It was as if someone famous was
going to a big event and had an entourage of body guards clearing
the way for them and when it was safe the movie star would then
appear. That was how it played out right there in my conservatory
and the best way I know of describing what happened.

I am not consciously aware of any message Mother Mary had
for me and I am still not too sure why she came to visit me that
day although she was, and still is, most welcome! In this physical
dimension of time and space the event did not seem to take very
long. And then, just as quickly as they came, they left in reverse
order of how they had appeared. Mother Mary went first and then
all of her angelic entourage closed in and left after her. I was left in
a state of bliss for the next three days that followed and continued
to go over the event in my mind. Below is the sketch that came
through the first time Mother Mary visited me.

"Mother Mary's Visit" © Michelle Rathore 2010

After I did a bit of research I found out that the three images are referred to as 'vesica pisces'. This is a very ancient symbol which one of its meanings refers to Jesus Christ and is a symbol of immense power and energy. Number three also being significant in that it refers to 'the trinity' which is the Father, Son and Holy Spirit. Three represents the mind, body and soul with the union of those three entities pretty much making up the total human being while still allowing for a connection back to the world of spirit. The mind completes the bridge connecting body to spirit. This mystical symbol is widely referred to as the junction of the dimension of the divine with the dimension of matter and the beginning of creation. The number three also refers to 'that which is holy' and I can clearly see why this symbol would come through just before and as Mother Mary appeared to me.

Anyone would have thought just having Mother Mary visit them *once* would have been the pinnacle of a lifetime! But I was again blessed with a visit a few years later (2013) while still living in the UK. I had become very ill due to stress from work demands. A friend living back in the United States had become aware that I was not well and offered to send me some distance healing. I happily accepted and then forgot all about the conversation. Two nights later as I was asleep in my bed, lying on my left side, facing the middle of the bed, I woke up as I was aware there was someone behind me in the room next to the bed. As I opened my eyes I was aware there was a stunning blue glow which seemed to emanate from behind me. The whole room was lit up and as I looked over my shoulder to the right I could see Mother Mary standing next to the bed with arms outstretched toward the ceiling. The blue color that flowed from her was the most magnificent shade of blue I have ever seen. Mother Mary's arms were open and outstretched toward the ceiling which had a vortex of energy powerfully swirling in the same blue color that radiated from Mother Mary's robes. She looked up into the vortex of energy which completely hid the ceiling. It was as if the ceiling had evaporated and there was just this amazing vortex of energy in its place. I was once again filled with peace and lay my head back down on the pillow falling into a very deep and restful sleep. That image of Mother Mary in my room that night has been forever etched in my mind as my new 'best memory'.

The next day I emailed my friend back in the USA. He relayed to me that he had requested Mother Mary's assistance, along with several other Masters, to aid in my healing process. I conveyed my amazing story of what had happened the night before and thanked my friend for their help. Requests for assistance are heard and always responded to. I already knew this before my visit from Mother Mary but now I am able to tell you for certain from an entirely different point of view. All of the Masters, Angels, Archangels, etc. in the hierarchy of God's highest light can hear you. All you have to do is ask one time with an earnest heart and your request is heard. Sometimes we don't always get exactly what we have asked for in exactly the way we asked for it to come to us but I truly know deep in my soul that Beings of Light, who are in service to the Divine Creator, work also for our highest good. Ask that what you want or need come to you for your highest good and then release your request to the powers that be – then look for the reply if it is not initially apparent. All prayers are answered and sometimes you will find that to not have your prayer answered was indeed the best solution anyway.

Within a day or so I was still so taken with the whole experience of having Mother Mary visit me again that I felt very drawn to paint her. Immediately her face emerged on to the canvas in what seemed such a very short time. This was perhaps only a half an hour or so. I can't quite recall even standing near the paints and materials sorting out what colors to use. It all just seemed to flow out onto the canvas as if my magic. Once there was just her face on the canvas – I stopped. I couldn't believe what I was seeing. She looked so beautiful to me and I decided to leave what had appeared on that massive canvas to dry. Over the next few days I would often go back into the studio to just sit and look at her face. The vision from the night of Mother Mary in my room would return to me over and over again while I considered all the possibilities of what had occurred that night. I desperately wanted to carry on painting the rest of the canvas but I was struck with fear that I would ruin what I had started. I didn't want to destroy the painting by carrying on without having fully considered how to proceed. I would sit and ask Mother Mary to tell me how to complete the painting. I would ask her if there was something in particular I was supposed to be bringing through for her. I really did obsess on not wanting to mess the painting up and found that I had completely stopped the painting at that point. This went on for a couple of weeks and then one night I had a conversation with my oldest son, P.J. I told P.J. about my fears and that I didn't want to ruin what I had started for Mother Mary and then with the wisdom that sometimes only your child can relate to you P.J. said to me, "Mom, I don't know why you are so apprehensive, she wouldn't have come to give you inspiration if she didn't think you were capable. Let her trust in you be a source of motivation, not anxiety."

I picked up the paintbrush the very next day and with renewed energy flowing through me once again continued working on the painting. While painting there were times I often felt almost hypnotized and would find myself saying 'Hail Mary's' as I sat face to face with Mother Mary. At one point I asked Mother Mary, "Mother what am I to call this painting?"

The answer seemed to float effortlessly from her consciousness into my own, "Unfinished Work. We both have that in common." And so the painting was named *Mother Mary – Contemplating Unfinished Work*. What happened next was almost incomprehensible to me. Even before I had completely finished the painting or even signed it I was contacted by a private collector asking if the painting of Mother Mary was for sale. I had shared a photo of the painting with friends on Facebook and the collector saw her there on my page. As it turns out we did come to an agreement and I came to understand that it was the perfect home for Mother Mary to go to although I have to admit that it was bittersweet packing her up for shipment and I did find myself wiping a tear or two on the day she was picked up for delivery. It was as if a little bit of my own soul was going too as I had quite enjoyed sitting in my studio 'talking' to Mother Mary. The rapid pace of the sale was like Mother Mary was telling me that not only did we have unfinished work but that she would be supporting me, literally, on that journey as well.

"...in an infinite universe, anything that could be imagined might somewhere exist."

—Dean Koontz, Dead and Alive
American Author (1945 -)

20. Sleepy Time with Spirit

As I have described in many chapters of this book spirit have been working with me in many different ways over the course of my life so far. Not only do they work with me while I am awake, but also when my body is sleeping. You see, the spirit inside our body does not need sleep. As our physical body sleeps our spirit gets up and goes about its business of learning while our body gets the much needed recharging it needs to keep going the next day. Over the years I have been able to figure out several types of occurrences which happen to me while my body is resting. Many people report these nightly happenings such as out of body experiences (OBE) and some call them astral traveling which is exactly what the name implies. Our spirit is traveling around on the astral plane which is another *unseen* dimension coexisting alongside our own third dimension of reality. A majority of people have no recollection of what they have been up to in the night once they wake up. Once they wake up the tasks involved in our daily living take over and their nocturnal ramblings are just so much fairy dust to them.While some of these nightly occurrences are most definitely happening on the etheric level as well as an alternate time line I will have to say that other times I am left wondering if I have had another prophetic dream such as the one that revealed my sister's upcoming auto accident and her death back in 1989.

Some people find it difficult to accept a 'future reading' , or to give one for that matter, as every choice we make going forward effects how our future will turn out. In fact, while I was going to the Spiritualist Church during part of my development phase, I was told it is not acceptable to give this type of reading as sometimes people will make the event happen instead of using the information wisely. This is not the purpose of showing someone the future if, indeed, you possess the gift of prophesies. You see, there are two ways to think about getting a reading regarding your upcoming future. On one hand you are shown what *might* happen if you continue living your life just as you are and make no conscious changes. On the other hand if you are told something which is not as favourable as you had hoped then you can make adjustments to try and avoid that situation altogether. Let's say you come to me for a reading and I tell you that Spirit is showing me an upcoming wedding for you or perhaps they show us a new baby on the way. Well, if you haven't got a boyfriend then you might say, "How can I get married and have a baby when I don't even have a boyfriend yet?" The obvious answer might be that you have a boyfriend on the way which will have the qualities you would like in a husband and when you do meet and fall head over heels in love it would be advisable to be careful in the baby making department as that is a very real possibility whether you had thought about it or not. Sometimes we just need to think things through and be smart and this is what Spirit might have been referring to in this instance. So if you had planned on turning your life to one of devotion and becoming a nun then you might want to think about how that is going to work out in your life for you. Maybe Spirit is trying to help you make some decisions that would affect your life and future happiness. Try to not make a future reading look black and white; there are always variables when it comes to planning out your future no matter what you *thought* you were going to be doing. Sometimes life has a way of taking you in directions you had never dreamed of.

So with that said I will share with you some of the nocturnal happenings which really stick with me to this day. Some people will say that I should not share with you one of these stories but you must be your own judge. I am not predicting these things will happen at some point in the future – I am merely sharing my experience with you in the hopes that should these same images be making their way to you then we might make some sense of it together. I won't be sharing with you what I call 'normal dreams' because, like everyone, I have those too. You know those dreams that just sort of help your mind sort out the Freudian part of your life. I know there are a great number of people who put a lot of stock in their dreams and all that they may hold. I am forever either saying or hearing someone say, "You will never guess what I dreamed last night!" And then go on to tell a long and twisting tale followed by what this or that may mean to them in their lives. The images or 'visions' I will share here have happened on the etheric plane, alternate time lines, during astral travel and perhaps as part of our ancient heritage of prophetic dreams as introduced throughout The Bible.

Triplehalos

One night in 2001 I was woke in the night needing a toilet run. Yes, this is glamorous stuff but a necessity to the story no less. It was during that time that my husband and I were going through a series of IVF treatments for our first child together. We had already endured two rounds of treatment including injections, pills, multiple doctor's visits, surgical procedures, ultrasounds and not to mention the most painful element of all - waiting, unsuccessfully and I was really becoming down heartened that I would never have another baby. It had been eighteen years since my little Marcus had passed away as a baby and with each passing year my hope faded a little bit more. So, I was in the dimly lit bedroom making my way to the bathroom just off the other side of our room. On my return trip to bed I had something catch my attention in the top right corner of the room. There were three perfect orbs of light shining as though they were each loaded with millions of stars and all hovering very tightly up in the corner of the room. I continued to stare at them for fear they would disappear. I was so amazed at how beautiful they were and I knew I was wide awake as I was standing next to the bed at this point. Slowly, I lay down on my side of the bed facing away – and thinking what to do next. I could hear Ajaz next to me still asleep. That man could sleep through a train wreck! I turned over and looked up at the corner of the room again. They were still there shining; the most magnificent sight I have ever seen up to that point in my life. I lay back down again with my mind racing. I wanted to know – what did they want? I was excited and a little spooked at the same time. We are always a little leery of things we don't quite understand but, I wasn't afraid by any means. I decided I would turn over one more time and if they were still there I was going to wake Ajaz up and show them to him. I turned over one more time and was very disappointed that they were now gone. I assumed my chance had passed to try to communicate with them and then I figured if they had wanted to say anything to me then they could have when I first saw them. Reluctantly, I turned back to my side of the bed and quickly fell into a deep sleep passing into the etheric. Now, I don't know what other people see but when I am here it looks like something I've seen in a movie before. Everything is very white and there is a mist all around. It's as though the air is alive with spirit. Some people use the term etheric and astral plane interchangeably. All I know is that it is when my consciousness is actually in the spirit world and I am fully aware of what is happening. Some people call this astral travel too.

As I arrived in the etheric I could see three spirits huddled in a circle having a deep discussion as though they were making some very important plans. I walked up to these three smaller (in size) spirits as I wanted to either hear what they were saying or be included in their discussion. As I got right up behind the one closest to me the spirit turned around and looked at me in the eyes. This spirit had the most intense blue eyes I have ever seen in my life. It was the only color among all this white mist and stuck out so intensely that I still have it etched in my memory today. It was at that point my spirit came back to my body and I woke up. I thought it was strange that I had three magnificent orbs of light in the room before I went to sleep and then I had a quick trip to spirit where I visited with three small spirit beings; one with piercing blue eyes. I was sure I would definitely find out what this all meant someday.

We continued going to our doctor's appointments and that very month we found out that on the third try with IVF we had been successful. After what seemed like the longest nine months in the history of pregnancies we finally had our lovely first daughter, Xara. Xara with the most piercing blues eyes I have only ever seen one other time; in the spirit world. Her twin brothers would follow two and a half years later just as though an important plan had all come together at last. I just know those three magnificent orbs of light which shined and twinkled like they were filled with millions of stars that night in my room are my three very special angels I refer to affectionately as my 'triple halos'.

The Spirit Library

I was in a huge mansion which appeared to be made of white marble. There were other people there too and we seemed to all be downstairs in a reception area waiting for something or someone.

I was then aware of being near the base of an upward winding staircase. A man came quickly from my left and immediately grabbed my attention with his sense of urgency. He reached out for my hand as though it was finally my turn to go somewhere and so I took his hand as he led me quickly up the stairs. He said, "I will take you to who you want to see - it's who they all want to see (referring to the others also waiting).

We quickly ascended the white marble staircase as though

flying and at the top of the stairs there was a very large, heavy, wooden door to which my escort went right to the door and opened it to let me in. The door swung open to reveal a room with a warm golden glow inside and had book upon book lining the shelves which went all around the walls. A being of light faced us and he looked quite pleased to see me. There was also a young person sitting at a small table facing away from me with paper and quill diligently working on writing something. As I entered the room the being made the gassho prayer gesture to me and I returned the same gesture to him. (Basically this means "the spirit in me salutes/recognises the spirit in you" and it is used to show respect for Buddha's, Bodhisattvas, Patriarchs & Teachers.)

At first the being seemed to be a glowing/holographic/3D spirit but as my eyes adjusted I could see the most amazing site. It was the outline of a person but without skin/hair or other human attributes. This being was full of billions of stars and galaxies and all knowledge - pure wisdom and truth. At the time it struck me that this Eternal Being might actually be a manifestation of God. Perhaps it was my higher self? He reached out and took my hand - I asked, "Please tell me what I am to do." Even in the vision my soul was reaching out for direction and guidance from this Eternal Being who seemed to encompass all knowledge and wisdom.

He turned and walked behind the young person at the table as though I was supposed to follow. Naturally I did and looked at what the youngster was writing but the letters were unfamiliar to me - a different, ancient looking language. It was almost like Greek writing or some other type of ancient codex unknown to me.

This being full of galaxies spoke to my mind, "He knows seven languages."

At hearing that my spirit shot right back into my body and I woke up with a gasp as though I had been under water for some time and needed to breathe oxygen back into every pore of my being. I laid there with the image frozen in my mind. These are the moments when I try the hardest to not forget anything I have witnessed and in the midst of replaying what I have just saw I also lay quietly trying to understand if there is more to come from any spirit that might still be in the room with me.

I have often wondered what knowledge I might gain from that cryptic message. I asked the Eternal Being to 'please tell me what I am to do' and the Being's reply was to show me a diligent student who was transcribing tomes and was doted on for knowing seven languages. I could take it literally and assume I am to start learning different languages. I can see how that might promote peace on this planet if we were all able to more readily understand each other. We could visit far off destinations and communicate with each other easily. We could develop friendships and a sense of understanding of other cultures which I am sure would lead to more love in the world. Or, was the student transcribing texts into different languages? I have a sentence on the bottom of my email signature that reads 'Educating oneself is the greatest responsibility there is.' Perhaps self-education and dedication to service are the messages here? Perhaps there are many messages and all apply.

Evil Being

Another night found me again in the ethers or in the spirit world as I like to think of it. I often go to sleep hoping I will again be allowed to remember when I have been 'over there' working or visiting as it really is a most amazing place to witness. I was fully aware of 'where' I was as it had the same familiar look and feel as it always did. Everything is all white and has a misty rolling effect around it. I believe this is just the energy of the ethers as everything is created out of this living material. I became aware, as I stood there, of a being which looked in solid form. It was not a being of light as I had previously encountered. This time the 'person' seemed to have an evil look on his face and he was pacing back and forth about 5 feet from me. He paced while he had pulled his arms behind his back and clasped his hands together as though in deep thought. Continuing to pace while looking at me - the evil smirk on his face told me that I was going to need help with this one! I watched wondering what this being wanted with me and what was he thinking so deeply about me for? I also wondered how this evil looking being could have been allowed to be in this place that I had only known as a place full of light filled beings. He appeared to be wearing a tight fitting waist coat along with tightly fitting leggings or trousers. His black hair was slicked back and slimy looking. Immediately, and without any hesitation, I called out for assistance, "ARCHANGEL MICHAEL!"That evil being stopped and glared at me but did not approach any closer. Instantly I felt a surge of energy which came down through the top of my head and seemed to move off to my right and yet out of my sight. The evil being looked in the direction of the energetic blast I had just felt and said, "Zadkiel?" and he smirked as he cocked his head sideways in amusement. Although I was very happy that someone had arrived to assist me I still made my petition again, "ARCHANGEL MICHAEL!" Instantaneously the same thing happened again. I felt a surge of energy burst down through the top of my head and out to my left this time – again out of my sight. The evil being again looked in the direction of the energy that had just come through me and again he smirked as he questioned, "Chamuel?" Immediately realizing that I had still not reached who I was calling I shouted again, "ARCHANGEL MICHAEL!" The same sequence of events followed for the third time. The same burst of energy came down through the top of my head and moved off to my right outside of my sight. This time the evil being looked in surprise and as he addressed our new addition he had a nervous looking smirk as he questioned, "Michael?"This time I felt the energy of Archangel Michael as he moved into the space in front of me blocking the evil being from my sight. It was at that time that I was sent back to my body and not allowed to witness whatever transpired between the evil being, Archangel Zadkiel, Archangel Chamuel and of course Archangel Michael. I knew I had needed help. I called for it and was blessed three times.

I don't know what that evil being was planning or if he was thinking up some great disaster to throw at me in the physical world but I do know this - whatever challenges you are facing in your life I hope you now understand that if you call out to God or his/her Messengers of Light that you are *always* heard and they *always* respond. You just have to ask.

Hospital Viewing Portal

Last year I had the most amazing vision but I'm not sure what plane of existence I should call this, if it actually has another name, as it felt more like an alternate time line to me and I sure hope it was too. I will tell you why. I was aware I was in the spirit world along with three other beings that seemed to know me quite intimately. We were standing near a very large full length window which seemed to be a viewing portal of some sort. It was as though it was a very large clear glass window and yet it was also like a full size monitor at the same time because we were looking at where (another place and time) I had just come from through this portal. We were looking at the front emergency entrance to a hospital. It was the emergency drop off point and I gathered I was taken there in my physical body but had not survived. All of these messages were coming very quickly and quite naturally straight into my head telepathically. We would look at each other and these thoughts would just fill my head and quite naturally I was able to send my thoughts to them as well.

One spirit sent me the thought, "They carved him from your belly. It was a boy and they named him Jonathan."

Very nonchalant I nodded an acceptance to their statement and my reply was, "I do seem to like that name; I gave it to another child I had too."

Then another spirit on the opposite side of me held up a

newspaper and for some reason I was drawn to the date. The year read 2047 and that is all I have been allowed to remember at this point. I was popped back into my sleeping body where I woke straight up.

Now, there are several ways I can think about this. If it was a prophet dream then I will die in childbirth in the year 2047. At the time of this writing I am 47 years old (2013) so I don't think there is any way I will be having another baby in the year 2047 at which time I will be 81 years old, that is, if I am still alive then! So, I think that pretty much rules this out as being a possible future for me in this lifetime.

The next feasible thing that I can think of would be that I could possibly die in the next 10 years, reincarnate quickly and still have time to grow up and die (again) in childbirth in the year 2047. I will try my hardest to not make this one happen!

And then there is another possibility that the vision I was shown was of an alternate time line completely. There is the chance that we are operating on many timelines and science has proven this more than once. This asks the question then is there a difference between alternate time lines and parallel dimensions/ universes? Are they similar but only to a certain degree and then become completely something else? I can only imagine that you can have many parallel universes with alternate time lines in each one making each universe separate and distinct but the alternate time lines are going on in that universe at exactly the same time but running alongside each one to produce a different outcome. In effect they share a certain part of their history until they split off to run side by side producing different outcomes. I saw a movie once that illustrated this idea quite nicely called *Sliding Doors* starring Gwyneth Paltrow.

So, there are my thoughts as to who or what that vision of the hospital viewing portal might mean for me in my either known or unknown future. You might ask why I was shown this if I don't have the ability to decipher it yet? My answer would be that we have been entering and undergoing a radical change in the history of humankind. We are actually making an evolutionary leap as we speak and it won't be measurable until enough people go through this phenomenon which some are calling a physical ascension. I see it because I can. It's that simple.

One Voice

There have been times I couldn't wait to go to bed because I was hoping to get to go back to one of the most beautiful places I have ever witnessed. This night as I arrived in the spirit world I was aware that I had found "my place" and settled in. I was an orb of light but very much aware that I could take form if I chose to. Staying an orb of light was just my natural form so this is the way I chose to be there hovering silently in this magnificent cathedral like area which was located way out in the deep universe. I saw that I took my place along with other orbs of light that seemed, from my perspective, to go on for an eternity in rows and rows as though taking our places in an enormous coliseum. There were roman type columns that hung in mid-air all around this cathedral which seemed to be a type of divider and give a feeling of defining the location we were at in some way. If I look up all I see is the deep universe twinkling around here and there which must be other planets far off but look like stars to me where I am. We are all facing the same direction which is toward an enormously bright light source. It is so bright I cannot look right at it because I will want to go *into* it if I do. Then I am aware of my own voice; I am singing one long constant note. I realise that we are all singing in unison that same note. Immediately I am consciously aware that I am now singing my own note – I can hear that I am separate now. As soon as this realisation hits me I am once again singing in unison with the other orbs of light. This continues to switch back and forth. I am me – I am one. We are all singing to the massive light ahead of us; joining our songs in praise and self-realisation. I understand this is my true home there out in the Universe – separate and yet one singing eternally and in communion with the Light.

Texas 2022

And so we arrive at the story some say I should not be telling you about. As I said previously I cannot say these things will come to pass. I am merely sharing my experiences with you in the hopes that if you are encountering the same phenomenon that I have been experiencing throughout my life then perhaps you will begin to stop and listen to what you are being shown as it may hold some significance in your life for you too.

I was on an aircraft of some sort but felt as though it was round and I could not see out of the windows mainly because there weren't any. There was a row of white seats around the perimeter of the white craft which also led to the feeling of being inside a round object. I was aware we were up in the clouds though and way up high. There was an older man there and I became aware, telepathically, that his name was Raymand or it was his nick name or something but the other's that were there kept referring to him as Raymand. It had a very hard sound to it like Ray-mand. I thought it was strange as I had not heard that name before. Then the lady next to me said, "You know he was the one working on Tesla?" and I seemed to know what that was and said, "Oh, really?" in a very interested sort of way. (I can tell you that before this event I didn't really know who or what "tesla" was.) Sometimes we act like we know what someone is saying to us without truly knowing *what* it is they are saying to us and this is what I was doing with this lady sat next to me.

Looking at the older "Raymand" he bashfully acknowledged he was the one they meant and he came over and began telling me about it (tesla) - he was sending me information to my mind but not speaking to me - so it seemed appropriate to ask him, "What can you tell me about the ET's and do you know when they will de-cloak their ships?" (I don't know why I asked him this!)

He said he was unsure of what he should tell me about that or if he should say anything about it at all but "they" did want me to know that Texas would no longer be on the map (speaking in terms of the future). So, I very calmly asked him "When will this happen?" And he quickly replied, "2022."

He seemed very nervous as though someone was listening to him and what he was saying to me. As a woman came walking up he got a bit nervous and, getting his items together that he had been showing me, slowly walked off and sat down in the seat he had been in to start with.

This woman who came up to me seemed to be someone I recognized – she was someone famous where she was from - but I couldn't place where I knew her from or who she really was - I just knew she was really famous. A very well-known and important figure perhaps there in the clouds? I noticed how emaciated she looked and she seemed to have clothes superimposed on her but I knew she wasn't wearing clothes – she was so skinny and had a pasty grey color to her skin. Indeed, thinking back, she looked like a grey alien with a hologram of clothing superimposed over her body as though I may need to see that to feel at ease in the situation. I thought at the time how strange it was that she had such thick hair. It seemed to be a wig and about 10 times too thick for the head of such an anorexic looking person. And it was cut in the Cleopatra haircut style. The other strange thing was that even though she was speaking to me (my mind) I couldn't see her face. There seemed to be a thick grey fog or mist where her face was but it didn't really bother me and I didn't ask her about it. She sat down across from me and asked me what was I working on right now? (meaning my projects) I looked down at my handbag and started going through it to find some examples of my work - it seemed important to her that I carry some things with me in case I needed to show them and she wanted to have a look and see what I had with me or what I was working on at this moment. She produced a big envelope which had loads of my paintings, drawings, etc., and started going through it while commenting, "Oh yes, that's fine...." and continued to look through the file of my work.

She then asked me if I had been talking to Raymand. I said, "Yes, do you know what he had worked on?"

She said, "Yes he was involved with Tesla energy." I said, "And he says that Texas will be off the map in 2022."

She said, "Yes, that's right."

I calmly and with a hushed voice said, "But, that's where all my family live." I was just hoping she could offer a bit more information about what was going to happen. Her very matter of fact reply to me was, "Yes, we know."

She then looked at me and said - referring to Raymand, "You know he died 2 years ago?"

I looked at her and immediately snapped right back into my body and sat right up in bed as though I had been under water for a very long time and needed to take a deep breath. I was wide awake!! I had to get up and go downstairs. I had to write it all down before I could go back to bed as I didn't want to forget any of it. My mind was racing with all the implications of what I had just witnessed. I kept telling myself that I knew it was not a 'dream' but one of those very real visions I have witnessed so many times in the past only to find them come true at some point in the future. I wrote it all down and then tried to go back to bed and get some sleep. I silently hoped I would resume the vision once more when I went back to sleep and perhaps be allowed to get the rest of the information that they may have been ready to give me just before I popped back into my body and woke up.

The next day I googled 'Tesla energy' and found out that it was developed in the 1930's and depending on how you viewed it – it was either a 'Death Ray' or a 'Peace Ray'. Perhaps that is why they were referring to the man as "Ray-Man" – I did feel at the time it was a nickname. I wonder if this Tesla Energy is a clue as to why Texas will be "off the map" in 2022? I have to wonder – what can "off the map" also refer to? Wikipedia © describe off the map "is an idiomatic or slang term which has been used to denote a place far removed from civilization, or to delineate a subject considered out of date, out of fashion, or consigned to oblivion." Since I am originally from Texas perhaps it means that Texas will be *off the map* for me in particular? Perhaps there will be a defining event in 2022 which will change my perception of Texas – forever.

Conclusion

What now? Seek and you shall find – but not always exactly what or where you think it will be or exactly in the place you should find it. The hardest part about seeking is being discerning and not just taking every answer that falls from the sky. Sometimes it's not the answers but the journey that's important. It's those people you meet along the way who add spice to your own flavor. It's being a student sometimes and being a teacher other times. It's listening more than talking and smiling more than crying. It's helping others without the thought of any reward in return. It's having compassion for someone who just needs a hug.

It seems like a very long time ago thinking back on it now. My journey has taken me to another continent – another world. That journey of blind faith which felt like an empty waste of energy sometimes and then other times it has been an absolute joy filled roller coaster ride of euphoria.

And, what was I looking for? And, where will I find it? Who will have the answers I seek? If, and when, I find that illustrious person will they be so benevolent as to share their wisdom with the likes of me? I wondered back then, in the beginning and I still wonder now. It doesn't matter how much I learn or what achievements I seem to make I know that it will never end. Living is learning. It's as simple as that. We must keep moving forward. We must keep helping those who have not managed to come up to our rung on the ladder yet. Because I am waiting for someone to grasp me firmly and tug me up to my next rung too!

At the beginning of this book I told you a story about Lizzie. She's the little girl who came to visit me while I cooked in the kitchen one day. I didn't know how I would ever be able to give her message to her mother. I understand now; spirit finds a way.

Looking back over my life I can tell you that all growing up I had this feeling of being special. I had (and still have) this feeling of being divinely guided. It's as though my every step is being shepherded by unseen hands. I have never walked alone. Everything always worked out for me no matter how difficult a situation I thought I was in. Lost items turned up in plain sight. People came into my existence that I needed. Sometimes they needed me. I don't know if it's because I am open to God's plan or if I am just floating along life letting it happen for my highest good. Maybe it's both. It was only after a string of unfortunate life events that I was really shaken to my core. I realized I was indeed human. Or, at least, I was having a human experience. I realized that I was not impervious to bad things happening to me. It was at that point that I went over the other edge a little and lost a bit of faith. I felt like a child who had been reprimanded unjustly and I took offence to it. I thought I had been abandoned at one point and it was at my very lowest point I realized that Spirit had never left me. It took a little one eyed girl searching for the light late one night to wake me up again. I had gotten too imbued in the physical world and lost touch with not just the spirit world but my own spiritual needs too. I had lost touch with my human heart. 'My amazing human heart.' This is where the spirit of God lives. My human heart had been touch by tragedy and I had closed it off so as not to have to deal with those horrors again. In doing so I had also cut off my connection to Spirit. I was suffering a self-inflicted spiritual death (separation). I did not want to play anymore. I caused myself to suffer because being away from our natural state of being is truly a torture. I know that may sound a bit cryptic as I have not put a lot of those stories in this book. There is more. There is always more to life than we see, hear – or feel and think.

If you have the urge to continue learning and seeking the truth, then do it. There is a reason. There is someone who is waiting to be given your message of hope. You are special and gifted even if you haven't exactly found your special place in the world yet. Keep going – you will find yourself and Spirit will be there the entire way with you – just like they have been with me.One last quote –

"Every day above ground is a good day."

—Nona Marie Swanson
(My grandmother)
(1918-1985)

I wish you great Joy & Peace on *your* sacred journey no matter what language you speak!

Shalom (לוסש), Namaste', Namo Amitofo, Walaikum Al-Salam, Salaamata, Peace, Pax, Achukma, Salam

Made in the USA
Lexington, KY
20 May 2014